Evidence for Joy

Unlocking the Secrets of Being Loved, Accepted and Secure

Josh McDowell
and
Dale Bellis

WORD BOOKS
PUBLISHER
WACO, TEXAS
A DIVISION OF
WORD, INCORPORATED

All Scripture quotations, unless otherwise identified, are from the New American Standard Bible, © The Lockman Foundation 1960, 1962, 1963, 1968, 1971, 1972, 1973, 1975, 1977. The Scripture quotation marked TLB is from *The Living Bible Paraphrased* (Wheaton, IL: Tyndale House Publishers, 1971); quotations marked KJV are from the King James Version of the Bible.

Library of Congress Cataloging in Publication Data

McDowell, Josh.
    Evidence for joy.

    Bibliography: p.
    1. Christian life—1960- . 2. Faith. 3. Apologetics—20th century. I. Bellis, Dale E., 1951-
II. Title.
BV4501.2.M4355   1984   248.4   84-11900
ISBN 0-8499-0400-5
ISBN 0-8499-2978-4 (pbk.)

Printed in the United States of America

First Printing, July 1984
Second Printing, September 1984

These things I have spoken to you, that My joy
may be in you, and that your joy may be made full.
—Jesus
John 15:11

CONTENTS

II. JOY MEANS BEING LOVED

III. JOY MEANS BEING ACCEPTED

IV. JOY MEANS BEING SECURE

PREFACE

My first contact with Josh McDowell was in September 1977. My brother Dave and I challenged Josh with a faith-stretching venture: develop a conference employing extensive multi-media resources to train laymen to use evidences for faith in their everyday life and witness. Eighteen months later we were on the road with Josh sharing with thousands of Christians life-changing truths on which to base not only their witness, but their life. We dubbed the weekend conference "Six Hours with Josh McDowell" and designed it to be a supplement to the ministry of pastors and churches in grounding believers in reasons why they believe and how that affects their practical walk with Christ. This book emerges from the message of that conference and attempts to wed the reasons for our faith with the reality of our walk. It's a challenge to live out the spiritual heritage that is already ours in Christ.

If you could spend days and weeks with Josh, as I have, you would find him to be a man of deep conviction and commitment. You would be ministered to most by Josh's commitment to his family—his wife, Dottie, and his three children. This is one of his main qualifications to minister with authority and integrity in the body of Christ. His books, tapes, films, TV specials, even the "Six Hours" conference—all are a direct outgrowth of Josh's commitment to be a godly husband and father. He serves as a model

11

for keeping the proper priority of the ministry: God, family, and ministry.

Would you like to know the secret of his commitment to his family? It lies in what Josh believes *about* God. Knowing the *who* and *what* about God produces a loving commitment to his wife and children. What do you mean? you might ask. At first you might think Josh's ministry runs on two separate tracks: his apologetic message—defending the faith on university campuses, writing books and doing research on Christian evidences; and his relationship message—sharing God's principles on love, sex, and marriage. But looking closer, you would find a definite relationship between evidence for faith and his messages on love, sex, dating, and marriage. The dynamic truth Josh shares on love relationships is a direct outflow of his deep convictions developed from *why* he trusts the God he serves.

As a young Christian in college and graduate school I toyed with apologetics as a fun intellectual pursuit. I read all I could get my hands on, jammed my academic schedule with extra classes, and relished the challenge of demolishing the objections of the occasional skeptic or ardent opponent of Christianity. Apologetics added to my arsenal of arguments for Christianity. But apologetics is not "ammunition" to use against the "enemy." It is often more useful to the believer than the unbeliever, answering nagging questions about the faith and producing boldness of witness. But it wasn't until after a few years of being involved in a practical ministry that I began to realize the vital link between knowing why I believe what I believe and living that out practically in my daily walk.

Josh and I were in Seattle together for one of the "Six Hours" conference events, and from the seed of a casual conversation there with him, this book was born. "Dale, why don't we write a book about how evidence for faith undergirds the answers to people's nitty-gritty needs?" Josh said. I agreed it was a good idea and felt honored at the opportunity to join him in communicating the message God was developing in both our lives.

This book can help you span the chasm between what you know

and how you live. You will soon find that we've not addressed every need possible, but we have tackled the most basic ones. You don't have many needs more basic than the needs of being loved, accepted, and secure.

This book is also a part of the supplemental curriculum to a six-part film series by Word, Inc., featuring Josh and titled "Evidence for Faith." You may have purchased this book in a bookstore or at a "Six Hours" conference, or received it as part of the film series instruction kit. There are several ways this book can be used. The leader's manual in the "Evidence for Faith" resource kit can help you select the best format for your study.

To make this book easier for you to read, except in this preface, the pronoun "I" will refer to Josh McDowell. Yet, unlike many books with co-authors, this was not written in an "as told to" style. And Josh and I have chosen to combine our experiences into composite illustrations to avoid the confusion of two voices speaking at once. It seemed simpler to have only one voice at a time.

A book like this one is a cooperative effort. Aside from my interaction with Josh on the manuscript, God has chosen to surround me with men and women suited to my needs, who motivate me to be the kind of man God wants me to be. Those who have "cooperated" in this project deserve special thanks. Chief among them is my dear wife, Brenda, along with our children, Robyn, Abby, and Matthew. They have freed their husband and father for the demanding task of communicating ideas in print. My senior advisor, confidant, and friend, Dave, who is far more than a brother, has labored long hours with me, steering this project through the maze of details from dream to reality. Special thanks go to Becky, whose care for detail goes a long way towards producing a typed manuscript. Joey Paul, vice-president, Educational Products Division of Word, Inc., has devoted himself beyond the call of duty to the completion of this project, along with Word editor Pat Wienandt, who has provided inestimably valuable counsel. Special thanks go also to Harold Fickett for his work in the final readying of the manuscript. My thanks ultimately go to God who has given me the opportunity to share with countless others the lessons He has been unfolding in my life for the past six years.

Salem, Ohio   DALE BELLIS
April 1984

INTRODUCTION

Does it trouble you that in the next 30 minutes, 285 children will become victims of broken homes; parents will beat, molest, or otherwise abuse 228 children; 685 teenagers will take some form of narcotics; and 57 kids will run away from their homes? Or that 5,000 new people each day will try cocaine?[1]

Those are staggering figures. Something has happened to the moral fabric of our society. It would be wonderful to say family, marital, and relational problems are limited to unbelievers. But they aren't. Many Christians, trying to cope in a society that has lost its bearings, are crumbling under the pressures of everyday life. More alarming is that the answers given to our problems are most often "whatever works for you." We live in an age characterized by "a crisis in authority." It is not that answers are not being given; it is that those answers are relative—the "it's right for him but not for me" syndrome.

In our society today, the traditional support systems, the very moral foundation to which earlier generations looked in times of crisis, have been undermined. Confidence in God and belief in the Scriptures, the church, moral absolutes, even the family and the institution of government, have been eroded. People no longer have the inner fortitude with which to resist life's pressures. Consequently, a generation has been set loose with no moral bearings.

All of this has affected the church. Divorce in the pew, as well as in the pulpit, skyrockets.[2] Sexual temptation and sin conquer and control once spiritually mature leaders.[3] Dottie and I have been shaken by the number of spiritual leaders who have called us for counsel in the last twelve months because their marriages are faltering. Our generation does not necessarily face more perplexing problems than generations of the past, but the foundations on which answers rest have been undermined. We face a crisis in authority.

This crisis has two fronts: first, the authority of the Bible as the inspired Word of God; and second, the Bible's practical authority in one's personal life. In this volume the focus will be on that second dimension.

Some great teaching exists today on the problems of marriage, sexuality, singleness, stress, child discipline, self-discipline, and church life. I am grateful to God for the strong expositors and Bible teachers He has raised up to minister to the Body of Christ today. Yet, regardless of the amount of fine teaching there is on the Bible, if there are questions, doubts, and suspicions about the *origin* of those teachings, they will not be applied. Questions about the validity and source of biblical truth undercut the authority of the teaching so that what remains are hollow, empty answers to some of life's pressing questions.

I am motivated to call fellow believers to consider the evidence that supports our belief in the trustworthiness, reliability, and authority of the Scriptures. The answers to our problems rest in knowing and applying the universal principles of God's Word. Unless we have solid evidence on which to accept the authority of Scripture, our foundation will continue to erode.

You may be unaware that my lecture series on the historical evidence for the reliability of the Scriptures has recently been adapted into a six-part film series called "Evidence for Faith," produced and released by Word, Inc., in Waco, Texas. The production of the film series was the culmination of six years of planning, prayer, and hard work. The evidence for the trustworthiness and reliability of the Scriptures has been presented in an appealing and usable way. While this book is distinct from that series, it *assumes* the evidence and facts of history presented in the films.

I say "assumes" because this volume builds on the evidence presented in the films and goes on to present what the Bible says about God, His trustworthy character, and His ability to meet all our needs. The film series presents evidence that the Word of God, our foundation, is a reliable and dependable document of history. This book presents evidence that God Himself can be relied upon and trusted.

For the purpose of this book, then, we need to distinguish between two types of evidence: evidence *for* God, the Bible, and Christ; and evidence *about* God, the Bible, and Christ. This book deals not with the evidence *for*, but with the evidence *about* God as revealed in His Word as a basis for faith. Both types of evidence are critical to know. On the one hand is the historical evidence and argument supporting the existence of God, the reliability of the Scriptures, and the claims of Christ, commonly known as apologetics. On the other hand is the biblical evidence about God's character, nature, and attributes as revealed in the Scriptures. In order to give an answer for why we believe and to reestablish the foundations of our faith (1 Pet. 3:15), we need to take into account both kinds of evidence. This book will not deal with the objective evidence and facts of history that convinced me God was real, that Christ was who He claimed, and that the Scriptures are trustworthy and historically accurate. I've written other volumes that set out that evidence.[4] We will be dealing with evidence about God and His character, and His acts in history, as revealed in the Scriptures, that demonstrate He is a God who desires to meet the deepest needs of His people.

As you know, the Bible is more than an accurate historical document. It reveals facts about God's nature, character, personality, and attributes that give unassailable reasons to trust Him for our daily problems. We will investigate some specific characteristics of God that will enable you to unlock the secrets to being loved, accepted, and secure by faith. The more you know about God, the more you will trust God. The more you trust Him, the more your needs will be met.

A fundamental premise underlies this book: God's principles of life are designed to lead you to maximum fulfillment. The more you align yourself with God's principles, the more abundant and joyful your life will be. This gives meaning to Jesus' words, "These things I have spoken to you that my *joy* may be in you, and that your *joy* may be made full" (John 15:11 emphasis mine). A careful reading of the Scripture supports the conviction that living life with a holy God results in tremendous joy. To live holy is to be happy. God's principles are designed with you in mind.

Evidence about God provides a basis for faith that meets your needs for being loved, accepted, and secure; and that kind of faith yields joy. The evidence presented in this book (as we have said) is facts, not *for* God, but *about* God, that serve as a basis for faith. After an introductory chapter in which I share my personal, spiritual quest as a skeptic, we examine true faith. Faith, based on the evidence of a trustworthy God, secures answers to your deepest needs. Faith must have an object, and the object of our faith is God and His inspired Word. The right view of God generates faith. The more we see God at work in our lives, the more we can be assured that He is worthy of our trust. There is nothing mysterious about faith. It is simply a matter of knowing the God we worship, knowing His holy, inspired Word, believing what He promises, and expecting the results of those promises.

Yet life is not always calm and peaceful. Our faith is challenged and tested. In chapter three we examine how a tested faith yields hope, a life characterized by the inner certainty of love, acceptance, and security; in a word, joy.

Then in parts two, three, and four we look specifically at how the evidence for God's trustworthiness enables you to be loved, accepted, and secure by faith. From personal examples as well as from a study of God's Word, you will discover how to appropriate the resources you *already* have in Christ.

The evidence in this book that God longs for you to live joyfully, as is the case with all other serious attempts to discover truth and apply it, needs to be uncovered and investigated. You will discover reasons you can freely trust Christ to fulfill your needs and enrich your life. But beware! You may learn something new about yourself. Apply what you learn and it will have a direct impact on your sense of being loved and loving others, your self-image, and security. If you have an honest heart, an appetite for truth and an openness to God's Spirit, you will be gratified by the results.

PART I

Faith Leads to
Joy

1

A Personal Quest

Do you get butterflies when you are asked to speak? Normally I don't any more, but this particular time was different. On a Wednesday afternoon I was to speak at a free speech platform, outdoors. I had been invited to Louisiana State University to deliver a three-night lecture series. During the day I spoke at the open air meeting. Louisiana State still has a "free speech" platform, popular during the student unrest days of the late '60s. From three to five on Wednesday afternoon everything stops. At a designated spot, nine speakers have ten minutes each to say anything they want. I spoke seventh in line. As I stepped to the platform, hundreds of students milled on the grass. Some were reading; others were tossing a football or throwing frisbees. In some cases, students yelled and screamed at speakers. In general, they paid no attention!

I stared at the crowd for a moment, and then said loudly, "Most of you here struggle with two fears."

In a matter of seconds, it was as if a "silence bomb" had hit the place. Everyone quieted. I couldn't believe it! Minutes before they had shouted, jeered and heckled each speaker. Now, everyone listened.

I continued, "One, you have the fear that you will never be loved, and two, the fear that you will never be able to love."

Absolute silence. Stares. They knew it was true.

Do you ever long to be loved with an unconditional, unstoppable love? Probably so. It's a desire felt by people of every culture, language and race. Why? Simple. You were created by God with the capacity to and the need for love. It was His idea. And furthermore, God designed it so He is the only source of satisfying that need. Here's even better news: He's promised to do it. How? With love, a love the Bible calls "agape" (a-ga-pay)—giving, sacrificial love. Your circumstances or your response to it do not matter. God keeps on loving you "in spite of." Unfortunately, not only at Louisiana State University, but in every metropolis, town, or village dotting this globe, men and women long for, but fear they'll never experience, that kind of deep, satisfying love.

But those nagging doubts about our ability to love and be loved are not our only problem. Let's be honest. Do you really like the person you are? If you do, count yourself fortunate. Most of us are suffering from a low self-image. And this is true regardless of the many excellent books addressing this need. Practical resources bursting with biblically sound teaching on personal acceptance and how to develop a positive self-image crowd Christians' shelves. Yet how much has your self-concept really been helped by these resources?

Psychology tells us that the way you view yourself is one of the hardest things for you to change. So many long to be at ease with themselves, to accept themselves, and they really try. But most of their attempts fail, and I think I know why. They have no real basis, strong evidence, if you will, for expecting their longing for acceptance to be fulfilled.

How do you define self-acceptance? To me, acceptance is knowing who you are, who made you who you are, and giving God the glory. You can be at ease with yourself when you *know God* has made you the unique person you are. Note the two italicized words in the previous sentence: *know* and *God*. That is the theme of this book—knowing God. Because knowing God will tell us all we need to know about ourselves. God's plans are perfect, so he must have known what he was doing when He made you. And you know what? He's not finished with you yet! So, don't get discouraged with flaws in your life, because the process of making you like Christ will take a lifetime. Your confidence in the design of the final product is in knowing *He's* in charge. You don't have to strain to be someone you're not. You can relax and be the person God made you while being thankful for the changes He is making in you. God is in charge of the process as well as the final product.

Unfortunately, it's one thing to believe in God's plan but another thing to live it. One reason this is so is because behind much of the disintegration of an individual's self-concept is another problem—a deep sense of insecurity, an inability to face life's crises with confidence and assurance. A deep vacuum of uncertainty fills many lives. Possessions, people, or power are some of the straws grasped to fill that void. Nothing seems to work. The pain persists.

Here again, knowing God provides the starting point from which the process of real Christian growth charts its journey. And in the matter of security, you start with who God is and what He is able to do for you. If security can be defined as that sense of confidence, assurance, and contentment with life that comes from knowing God, through Christ, personally, then being really convinced, mentally and emotionally, that God *is* in control of your life brings contentment with the outcome.

MY SEARCH

Tragically, I stumbled through life for years not knowing God. So my deepest longings for love, acceptance, and security went unfulfilled. As a non-Christian at Kellogg College, my goal in life was to be one of the happiest individuals in the entire world. Thomas Aquinas wrote: "There is within every soul a thirst for happiness and meaning." I wanted answers to questions: "Who am I?" "What am I?" "Why in the world am I here?" "Where am I going?" I wanted to be loved; I wanted to be accepted; I wanted to face life with confidence and security. And during my college years I set out on a search to discover the truth about life, about religion, about Christianity. I was empty inside. I wanted purpose in life.[1]

When I remember my childhood growing up on a 150-acre dairy

farm near Union City, Michigan, the happy times that come to mind are when I went fishing with my friend Dave in the creek that ran by our house or boating with my uncle on Rose Lake. But the childhood memories most vivid in my mind are the ego-shattering experiences which were part of my everyday existence.

I am naturally left-handed, but as a grade-school child I was forced by my teachers to change from being left-handed to being right-handed. One teacher, Mrs. Duel, stood over me with a ruler to slap my left hand if I reached out for anything with it. "Think, Josh," she would say. "Use your right hand!" I came to believe that left-handedness was inferior to right-handedness, and therefore I was inferior. As a result of my feelings of inferiority and the nervousness created by such treatment, I developed a speech impediment. My poor self-image and low self-esteem were compounded by my inability to speak properly. Not only did I feel clumsy and inadequate, but now stupid as well as I struggled to speak in front of my peers when called on in class.

Even some of my friends seemed to be as insecure and unable to succeed as I was. I recall a red-headed firebreather named Jerry who lived near our two-story wood frame farmhouse. Anything could make Jerry mad. His patience was very thin. Jerry would try to help his dad with the work around the house, and on many occasions his dad would say, "Jerry, you can't do anything right!" It did seem to be true. Jerry would try and put a screw in a hole, and if it didn't go in the first time he would lose his temper, jam the screw and strip the threads. Then it would never work, which made him madder. I remember building a "fort" together with Jerry in the woods behind our house. We imagined it to be our last defense against marauding savages and we were the last hope of protection for the civilized world. We had to build our fort fast! In his fury, if a pole wouldn't fit, or a nail bent, Jerry would yell, "I can't do anything right." Jerry grew up believing he was what his dad thought of him—an incompetent, mistake-prone clod. What child wouldn't believe his mom and dad? Or his teacher? Who else can he trust? Needless to say, Jerry and I never finished the fort.

And yet, these painful memories do not compare with the devastation caused in my life by my father. To me he was the town alcoholic. Union City is a small town of several thousand people. Everyone knew everyone else and everyone knew my father. My friends in high school made jokes about him. They didn't think it bothered me. I laughed on the outside, but cried on the inside. Sometimes I'd go out in the barn and see my mother lying in the manure behind the cows, beaten so badly she couldn't get up. How I hated my father for his cruelty to her! The only sense of security and stability I had as a child came from my mother's constant love. No matter where I had been or how early or late I came home, my mother always seemed to be there waiting for me. To vent my anger against my father and to avenge his mistreatment of my mother, I would try to humiliate him. If I knew my friends would be coming to the house, if my father was drunk, I would tie him up in the barn, and park the car up around the silo. I would tell my friends he was gone. I don't think anyone could have hated anyone more than I hated him.

The emotional insecurity and turmoil of my high school years set the stage for the search for meaning in my life I was to undertake during college. Although the big questions were as yet unarticulated in my mind, I was emotionally and spiritually bankrupt. I longed to be loved with an unconditional, unstoppable love. I wanted to be accepted by others, but more than this, I needed to be able to accept myself, to overcome my feelings of self-hatred. I wanted security, that sense of confidence that would allow me to live life with a peaceful heart and mind.

As high school graduation neared I looked forward to the freedom I would experience at college. No longer would there be the stigma of being the son of the town drunk. I could be a new person, my own person. I would find meaning for my life and, above all, happiness. When I began to look around me, it seemed that the most likely place to turn for answers was religion. Almost everyone I knew was into some sort of "religion," so I did the obvious thing and went to church. I went in the morning, I went in the afternoon, and I went in the evening. But there was no joy for me in church.

I felt worse inside the church than I did outside. All the while, I focused my attention on *my* efforts. As a result, my "believing" became performance-based. I thought approval could be won from God and others by my piety. But what a disappointment. "Religion" was clearly not the answer I was looking for.

During my freshman year at college I began to wonder if the answers to my need for being loved, accepted, and secure were in prestige. Becoming a leader, giving myself to a "cause," and being known on campus might possibly be the route to happiness. At college the student government leaders held the purse strings and threw their weight around. It seemed to me an attractive position to be in, so I ran for freshman class president and was elected. My ego was boosted by knowing everyone on campus and hearing, "Hi, Josh," from others. It was great making important decisions such as choosing which outside speakers to invite to campus; I spent the university's and the students' money to get the speakers I wanted. I threw more parties with student money than anyone else. But my happiness, like the happiness of so many others, depended upon my own circumstances. If things were going great, I felt great. When things would go lousy, I felt lousy. I would wake up Monday morning, usually with a headache from the activities of the night before, and my attitude was, "Well, here go another five days." I endured the routine of Monday through Friday, but happiness revolved around three nights a week: Friday, Saturday, and Sunday. Then the vicious cycle would begin all over again.

But there didn't seem to be anyone living any differently, or anyone who could tell me how to change the path of my downward spiral into despair and bitterness. Despite great frustration, there was a sincerity in my search for answers to life's important questions: "Who am I?" "Why am I here?" "Where am I going?"

As weeks went by, I began to notice on campus a small group of people: eight students and two faculty members. There was something different about their lives. They seemed to know why they believed what they believed. I enjoy being around people like that. Whether I agree with them or not, I admire a man or woman with conviction. The people in this small group seemed to know where they were going. That's unusual among many university students. I noticed that more than just talking about love, they went out of their way to help others. Their happiness was not dependent on circumstances; rather, they seemed to rise above flat bicycle tires, tough exams, demanding professors, lost football tickets and rude dorm mates. They had an inner source of constant joy, love and security. They had something I didn't have.

Like the average student, when somebody had something I didn't have, I wanted it. So. I decided to make friends with these intriguing people.

Two weeks later we were all sitting around a table in the student union. After a few moments of casual conversation, one student mentioned God. Now let's face it, if you're an insecure person and a conversation centers on God, you tend to get a little uneasy and try to put on a big front. Every campus, business office, or community has a big mouth, a person who says, "Aw, come on. . . Christianity, ha! That's for the weaklings; it's not intellectual."

Well, I put on the "big front." I looked over at one of the students, nonchalantly leaned back in my chair, and said, "Tell me, what changed your lives? Why are your lives so different from those of the other students, the leaders on campus, the professors?"

That young woman looked me straight in the eye and said two words I never thought I'd hear uttered with respect at that university. She said, "Jesus Christ." I said, "Oh, for heaven's sake, don't give me that garbage. I'm fed up with religion; I'm fed up with the church; I'm fed up with the Bible. Don't give me that garbage about religion." She shot back, "Mister, I didn't say religion; I said Jesus Christ."

I apologized for my attitude and then they challenged me intellectually to examine the claim that Jesus Christ is God's Son; that taking on human flesh, He lived among real men and women and died on the cross for the sins of mankind; that He was buried and He arose three days later; and that He could change a person's life in the twentieth century.

These people challenged me again and again. Finally I accepted their challenge, but out of the wrong motive. Rather than desiring

to learn the truth about Christianity, I wanted to refute its claims.
I didn't know there were undeniable facts; I didn't know there
was evidence to be evaluated; I didn't know there were reasons
why I could know for certain that I was loved, accepted, and secure.

So, I set out to intellectually refute Christianity. After two years
of research, the whole plan backfired on me. The evidence I uncovered convinced me Jesus Christ *was* who He claimed to be—the
Son of God, the Savior of the world. After an intense personal
struggle, I committed my life to Christ. And for the past twenty-
five years I have been sharing the joy of that love relationship
with all who would listen.

Christ changed my life. When I trusted Christ as Savior, I re-
ceived the love, acceptance, and security I had sought for so long.
Where there was hatred He gave love. Where there was rejection
He gave acceptance. Where there was insecurity He gave security.
Through my search for faith in Christ I found an intelligent basis
on which to have my deepest needs fully met.

A STRUGGLE WITH MISCONCEPTIONS

I might not have struggled so long in coming to Christ if I
had not had some crucial misconceptions about the Christian faith
in general and Jesus Christ in particular. This was a result of my
secular, non-Christian world-view. I didn't know that Christ either
desired to meet or was capable of meeting my needs, nor did I
realize that faith in Christ was my only hope for being loved,
accepted, and secure. Specifically, three basic misconceptions pre-
vented me from acknowledging Christ as my Savior and examining
His plan for meeting my needs. My quest, fortunately, forced me
to examine my assumptions about faith and resolve each misconception.

My first misconception was that Christianity was merely a system
of beliefs to adhere to or a set of theological propositions to live
by, rather than faith in a person, Jesus Christ. I didn't understand
that Christ desired an intimate love relationship with me by faith.

Secondly, I thought that before faith could be of any value one needed to have a lot of it. I strove for more and more faith. My attitude was, "It doesn't matter what you believe, just so you believe it enough and you're sincere." Thirdly, I thought faith didn't need evidence, that faith was blind. I reasoned that if faith needed proof then it couldn't be faith.

Little by little, and after much resistance, my first misconception was resolved. I began to see the truth about Christ. As I let down the false intellectual and emotional barriers I had built around me I became convinced by the evidence uncovered that Jesus Christ *was* who He claimed to be—the Son of God.

I began to understand the biblical concept of faith. I learned that a proper faith was directed to God and what He thought of me. It dawned on me that the key to faith was not how much faith I had, but in whom I had faith—Jesus Christ. I began to view myself as God viewed me—as an accepted, valued person of God's creation, righteous before God in Christ. I was accepted by God, not as a result of something I did, but because of who Christ is and what He accomplished on the cross for me. I learned I didn't need, nor could I attain, "great faith"; I only needed faith in a *great* God.

As a result of my faith in Christ, I came to understand that in God's eyes my worth and acceptance had already been won for me, based on my identification with Christ. Regardless of what people thought of me, or how I was influenced to view myself, there was a whole new basis for being and feeling accepted.

THE REAL PROBLEM

Christ can be trusted to keep His Word that He will exchange our drab existence for joyous living, abundant life! And while true love, total acceptance and complete security are rare in our frantic world, the biblical evidence that our desires in these areas will be fulfilled in Christ is abundant.

Then what's the problem? Why are people's needs not fully

met in these areas? It is because so many do not understand the basis for our faith in Christ to meet these deep needs. Without the evidence of Christ's trustworthiness, and the record of God's faithfulness in the past, we have no basis on which to appropriate God's power in our lives. Faith without evidence is no faith at all; it has no reason to trust God. Faith is not faith in the biblical sense unless it is based on reasons and evidence of God's trustworthiness. Faith must rest on facts and evidence that make that exercise of faith valid; otherwise we have no right to our faith. Faith is only as valid as the object in which it's placed.

Because faith needs reasons to exist, we must examine the character of the person we trust. If we are to have our needs met in Christ, what is the basis for that expectation? Is Christ worthy of my trust?

2

Does Faith Need Reasons?

A story is told of the days when the circus was a rare treat in most communities and individual acts toured the country making appearances in towns omitted from the main circus schedule. One daring tightrope walker breezed into a little town and rigged up a taut rope hundreds of feet above a rushing river. He dazzled the crowd by his talent and daring. Soon news of his prowess swept the little town and surrounding communities, and hundreds turned out to watch him accomplish his feats. He added chairs, wheelbarrows, and bicycles to his act.

After everyone seemed to be convinced of his ability, the tightrope walker addressed the crowd. "You've watched me walk on this rope across the river several times now. I've done it on my hands, while running, while riding a bicycle, even while pushing a wheelbarrow. Yet I have one last feat I want to accomplish. I want to push the wheelbarrow across on the rope with a person in it. Do you think I can do it?"

"Yes, yes," came the confident reply. "We believe you can do it."

"That's marvelous. As long as you have faith in my ability to do it, why don't you do this? I'll take the wheelbarrow up and each of you get in it one at a time and I'll wheel you across."

Silence. No takers.

Then from the back of the crowd a young lady spoke up. "I'll do it," she volunteered. "I believe in you."

With bated breath, the crowd watched the stunt man successfully complete his amazing "wheelbarrow walk." A reporter accosted the young lady.

"What on earth caused you to do that? Weren't you frightened?"

The young lady smiled with assurance, "Not really. That's my father and I've done this with him all my life."[1]

The young lady's confidence came from personal acquaintance with her father, the tightrope walker. She knew his qualifications, had watched him perform successfully all her life, and had experienced firsthand his acrobatic abilities.

So it is with your faith in God. The more you know why God and His Son can be trusted, the more assured you will be God keeps His promises. Based upon your developing acquaintance with Christ, the facts you know about Him and His faithfulness in your life and the lives of others in the past, the more reason you have to trust Him.

Yet, very few Christians can explain clearly what makes God worthy of their trust. They know they trust Him, but can't articulate why they do. In contrast, when the Bible asserts God's trustworthiness, it cites specific characteristics of God's nature qualifying Him to be trusted.[2] Abraham, for example, left his home town, Ur of the Chaldees, on the promise from God of a land, an heir, a nation and a blessing that was to extend to all the other nations of the world. *God kept His Word.* Daniel, as a young Jewish lad, was taken captive to Babylon where he quickly distinguished himself as a man of outstanding wisdom and insight. Daniel trusted specifically in *God's wisdom* and was able to interpret the King's mysterious dream (Dan. 2:20, 30). Gideon was called upon to lead a small army of untrained soldiers to defeat Israel's most feared enemy, Midian. He trusted specifically in *God's power* and routed the enemy (Judg. 7:22). Job, the proverbial sufferer, lost every good thing in life: family, possessions, health. By specifically acknowledging *God's control,* Job climbed from his pit of sorrow to reaffirm God's ultimate control over his life (Job 37–42). These great men did not exercise a blind faith in God. They exercised an intelligent trust because they were intimately acquainted with God and knew

Him to be faithful, wise, powerful, and in control. They knew what He was like.

Similarly, by specifically identifying those qualities of God that make Him worthy of trust, you too can be equipped to enjoy the abundant life God has provided for you. The specific characteristics that make God worthy of trust fall into two categories: His perfect character and unfailing performance.

THE TRUSTWORTHINESS OF GOD'S CHARACTER

Recounting the attributes of God and seeing the evidence of those attributes in your own experiences will increase your confidence in God. What are some attributes of God which you can point to in your own life?

God never changes. This is what many people mean when they say, "God has never failed me yet." Heaven and earth will pass away, but God is unchanging and certain. ". . . Christ is the same yesterday and today, yes and forever" (Heb. 13:8).

God is always right. He'll never do wrong. God can be trusted because He always acts consistently with His nature as God. God's character sets the rule for all right behavior. A brief statement the Apostle Paul makes, almost as a sideline as if it is so obvious it doesn't require explanation, is significant here. ". . . He cannot deny Himself" (2 Tim. 2:13). God cannot act contrary to His nature. It's the same idea as our word "integrity." Integrity is a firm adherence to a code of moral values. God's integrity flows out of His character as God, the absolute definition of right. For you or me to be trustworthy, we must have a basic set of moral values and then live by them consistently.

God is faithful. Hebrews tells us, "When God made the promise to Abraham, since He could swear by no one greater, He swore by Himself" (Heb. 6:13). God removed all doubt about His faithfulness by offering two reasons to trust Him: the unchangeableness of His promise (God can't lie) and the unchangeableness of His nature as God. And now, through Christ, God has overcome every obstacle to fulfilling His promises. In Christ, God's promises are a big "yes." "For as many as may be the promises of God, in Him they are yes; wherefore also by Him is our Amen to the glory of God through us" (2 Cor. 1:20). A God who loves us so much that He gave His only Son to die for us is quite certain to fulfill every promise He ever made. Jesus Christ is God's personal guarantee that the greatest and the least of His promises are true.

When it comes to your faith in Christ, you can explain why you trust *Him* by acquainting someone with the qualities of His character. You know Him. He's trustworthy. His actions always conform to His holy nature. His character is the final, absolute standard for right behavior. He can't do otherwise. Because He is God, He'll come through every time. You can count on it. In fact, the more you know Him the more confident you are He'll keep His Word.

While in South Africa sharing reasons and evidence for the Christian faith to the Muslims, I became even more aware of their contrasting concept of God. In one of my talks I made the point about the consistency of the character of God: He always acts according to His righteous nature. God cannot lie, because God is truth. God cannot steal and cheat because He is unselfish and holy. What He *does* is always consistent with what He *is*. God's consistency comes from His unchanging character of rightness.

After the talk, a young Muslim said, "Your concept of God is not my concept of Allah. Allah is 'all-powerful.' Allah's 'powers' can allow him to do anything." I said, "Can Allah lie and cheat?" "Sure," he responded. "Allah can do all things. He is not limited like your God. If Allah wants to love, he loves. If he wants to hate, he hates. Allah is 'all-powerful.'"

I asked him, "Could Allah punish you for something you did, even if it were good?"

"If Allah did not like it, he would punish me," came the reply. I went on, "Then you don't always know how Allah would respond, do you?"

He thought for a moment, then said, "No, I don't always know what he would do, but I do know he is 'all-powerful,' " he quickly added.

I nodded and went on, "You see, if I served Allah I would be serving him out of fear. If he exercised the 'power' to do wrong as well as right, simply because he desired to, he would be punishing me from his own selfish desires. That would be a dreadful motivation from which to serve God, because I would never know what angered him. Try as I might I could never please Him."

Since he was listening intently, I continued. "You see, I serve God out of love. God, being holy and perfect, establishes morality on the basis of love because He always acts consistently with His nature. I always know what angers God and I always know what pleases Him. You see, if I loved you and then beat you up and stole your money, would you believe I loved you?"

He didn't answer, but the question in his face told me he was confused. The power of God Yahweh to love perfectly does not limit His powers, but rather establishes His greatness. Our God is consistent and that means His actions always conform to His righteous character.

But there's a second dimension to God's greatness that qualifies Him to be trusted: His ability.

THE TRUSTWORTHINESS OF GOD'S PERFORMANCE

Someone may make a promise, desire to fulfill it, and not be able to fulfill that promise simply because of circumstances beyond his or her control. The reason may be legitimate, but the promise is still unfulfilled.

God is perfect. God not only has the integrity necessary to be trusted, He also has the ability to perform perfectly. Otherwise He is not completely worthy of my trust. Perfect performance is a requirement of total trustworthiness.

I have a dear friend with whom I enjoy hunting, boating, fishing, and other forms of relaxation. I have learned over the years that

I can always count on him—count on him to be late! I've learned
to compensate for his tardiness, but in our early friendship it was
a source of irritation. It is always those "extenuating circumstances,"
situations "beyond my control," which cause his consistent delays.
His intentions are pure although his performance fails.

Some of the excuses my "late" friend has given go about like
this: "I didn't remember our departure time was at 6:00 A.M.!"
His mind wasn't perfect, I couldn't fault him for that.

"I couldn't load up that fast. I'm not Superman, you know!"
He had his physical limitations, I couldn't fault him for that.

"Hey, come on, I couldn't help it! A slow moving train held
me up for twenty minutes!" He doesn't control Amtrak; I couldn't
fault him for that.

Intentions to keep a promise must be backed up with performance. The ability to perform perfectly 100 percent of the time,
under every conceivable circumstance, would require infinite qualifications—like God!

God is all-powerful. It is God's omnipotence that makes possible
perfect performance under every conceivable circumstance. When
God makes a promise He accomplishes His purpose through the
power of His Word. "So shall My word be which goes forth from
My mouth; it shall not return to Me empty without accomplishing
what I desire, and without succeeding in the matter for which I
sent it" (Isa. 55:11).

Therefore, you can have confidence in God, knowing His characteristics are unchangeableness, righteousness, faithfulness, perfection, and omnipotence. Your faith in God is grounded in your
knowledge of who He is, what He has promised, and what He
can do in your life. Knowing and feeling you're loved, accepted,
and secure is actually an adventure into a personal acquaintance
with Jesus Christ. As you become more deeply acquainted with
Christ, you learn of His qualifications. As you discover His qualifications, you trust Him even more. It's a cycle: the more you know
Him, the more you trust Him; the more you trust Him, the more
you will know and experience the present reality of your needs
being met.

The Apostle Paul says, "For this reason I also suffer these things, but I am not ashamed; for *I know whom I have believed* and I am *convinced* that He is able to guard what I have entrusted to Him until that day" (2 Tim. 1:12, emphasis mine). Paul shared his testimony six times in the New Testament, sharing what he believed, who he believed, why he believed, and the results in his life. Paul did this because it helped others to understand why his trust was in Christ and not someone else. Paul based his faith, and subsequently his eternal destiny, on the character and integrity of the Person he trusted. No wonder he had such an insatiable appetite to know Christ: "that I may know Him, and the power of His resurrection and the fellowship of His suffering, being conformed to His death" (Phil. 3:10). The more Paul knew and trusted Christ, the more his needs were met and Christ was glorified.

BUILDING A CONFIDENT FAITH

But, how can you acquire a confidence like that of Paul? How can you find all of your needs met in Christ? Well, first you must look into God's Word regarding your position in Christ.

So many Christians I've met don't know the birthright they have in Christ. Others simply haven't learned to lay claim to God's promises. Knowing *why* you believe *what* you believe will enable you to know not only what Christ has done for you in the past but what He can do for you now. And, more important, it will allow you to experience the reality of being loved, accepted, and secure that you already have in Christ.

You are complete in Christ. Even a quick reading of the Scriptures, especially the New Testament, will reveal that at the moment you trust Christ you have a relationship with God and are complete in Christ with all your needs met. Two passages from the Epistles of Paul teach this.

Paul introduces his letter to the Ephesians in words that set the theme for the entire book: "Blessed be the God and Father of our Lord Jesus Christ, *who has blessed us with every spiritual blessing in the heavenly places in Christ"* (Eph. 1:3, emphasis mine). Already, through Christ, you possess all spiritual blessings. They are yours. If you have Christ you have everything you need.

Paul spends the first half of Ephesians, chapters 1–3, explaining those spiritual blessings, and the last half, chapters 4–6, explaining how to practically live out those spiritual blessings.

Appropriate your spiritual blessings. If you are complete in Christ, nothing remains for you to receive. All that you need for joyful, abundant living is found in Christ. You need only to appropriate your spiritual blessings through faith. This glorious and wondrous truth is expressed by Paul to the Colossian church in more detail.

> This is what I have asked of God for you: that you will be encouraged and knit together by strong ties of love, and that you will have the rich experience of knowing Christ with real certainty and clear understanding. *For God's secret plan, now at last made known, is Christ himself.* In him lie hidden all the mighty, untapped treasures of wisdom and knowledge. . . .
>
> And now just as you trusted Christ to save you, trust him, too, for each day's problems; live in vital union with him. Let your roots grow down into him and draw up nourishment from him. See that you go on growing in the Lord, and become strong and vigorous in the truth you were taught. Let your lives overflow with joy and thanksgiving for all he has done. . . .
>
> For in Christ there is all of God in a human body; *so you have everything when you have Christ,* and you are filled with God through your union with Christ. He is the highest Ruler, with authority over every other power.
>
> When you came to Christ he set you free from your evil desires, not by a bodily operation of circumcision but by a spiritual operation, the baptism of your souls. For in baptism you see how your old, evil nature died with him and was buried with him; and then you came up out of death with him into a new life because you trusted the Word of the mighty God who raised Christ from the dead.
>
> You were dead in sins, and your sinful desires were not yet cut away. Then he gave you a share in the very life of Christ, for he forgave all your sins, and blotted out the charges proved against you, the list of his commandments which you had not obeyed. He took

this list of sins and destroyed it by nailing it to Christ's cross. In this way God took away Satan's power to accuse you of sin, and God openly displayed to the whole world Christ's triumph at the cross where your sins were all taken away (Col. 2:2–3, 6–7, 9–15, TLB, emphasis mine).

All that you need is to be found in Christ and nowhere else.
Faith is the key. Faith is at the root of appropriating those spiritual blessings you already have in Christ. Faith seizes and makes experiential what is already yours in Christ potentially. Faith brings down to earth in actuality what is true of you in the heavenlies (Eph. 1:3). Faith meets you where you are with your hurts, frustrations, and even anguish.

Faith in Christ is tied to two issues: (1) Christ is who He claimed to be (and who the Bible teaches He is), and (2) Christ did what He claimed He would do.

If the Bible is what it declares itself to be and if Jesus is who He claimed to be, *then* by faith you can lay claim to the resources in Christ for joyful living. By faith you know that His death on the cross was a sufficient sacrifice to God for the atonement of your sins and the sins of the world, that He conquered death by rising from that grave, and that He seated Himself at the right hand of God, confirming that you are accepted, forgiven, and redeemed. If Christ is who He claimed to be, then by faith you can know that all your needs for abundant life here and in the life to come are met in Christ.

Consider this list of some of the most basic needs you have as persons made in the image of God: love, acceptance, security, significance, purpose, forgiveness, competence. How does faith in Christ supply each one of these needs?

IF Christ is who He claimed to be, THEN by faith you know you are:

Loved. God demonstrated His love in history by sending His Son Jesus to die for you on the cross. Your faith doesn't produce God's love; faith simply possesses the love God has for you.

Accepted. Because of Christ's substitutionary atonement you are acceptable to God. He accepts you completely, without reservation, from the moment you trusted Christ as your Savior. God has revealed that the death of His Son on the cross broke down the barrier between you and God and won your acceptance. Your faith doesn't accomplish your acceptance; faith simply accepts your acceptance in Christ.

Secure. Because God loves and accepts you, He is working all things together for your good and His glory. God controls the affairs of your life and He is working out His perfect plan for you. Your faith doesn't cause you to feel secure; faith simply acquires the security you have in Christ.

Significant. Because God made you, He imparted His image to you, making you inherently valuable and important. The very act of Christ's death on the cross signifies your importance. Your faith doesn't make you significant; faith simply agrees with God's evaluation of your importance.

Destined. The Bible reveals that you were created to glorify God and to fellowship with Him. He redeemed you for the purpose of being His ambassador to carry the Gospel to the world. Your faith doesn't create purpose; faith simply rests in God's ultimate plan of universal restoration, enabling you to realize your destiny.

Forgiven. Christ's death on the cross is an objective statement that you are forgiven. Your faith doesn't save you; faith simply is the arm that reaches out to accept the forgiving grace God has for you.

Competent. God never calls you to do anything that He hasn't already endowed you with natural abilities or by spiritual gifts to do. The Holy Spirit is God's personal agent for empowering you to accomplish His work. Your faith isn't the power; faith simply connects you to the power source.

The abundant life is in Christ, not in you. Paul experienced such a life and expressed it this way: "I have been crucified with

Christ; and it is no longer I who live, but Christ lives in me; and the life which I now live in the flesh I live by faith in the Son of God, who loved me, and delivered Himself up for me" (Gal. 2:20). You see, it is knowing why you believe Christ that enables you to experience both in your mind and emotions what God says is already true of you.

How knowing why you believe relates believing to living can perhaps be further illustrated this way. I am dazzled by princesses, queens, monarchs, and all that goes with a royal kingdom. It's the child in me, I guess, a hangover from Disneyland story books. I must confess, I wanted to attend the royal wedding of Prince Charles and Lady Di, but had no hope my wish would come true. My wife was so enchanted by the prospect of a Cinderella-dream-come-true wedding that she got up at 4:00 A.M. to watch the gala occasion by satellite. I didn't have *that* kind of commitment! Dottie and I had little reason to expect a personal invitation to attend the wedding.

But suppose one evening while opening our mail we were to find a personal letter from the Queen of England among the postal circulars and bills from Penney's and Sears. She has invited us to the royal wedding of her son, Prince Charles, at St. Paul's in London! The letter is personally signed by the queen and sealed with the royal seal. A phone call from the British Embassy confirms the authenticity of the letter.

The queen's letter explains she has ordered her royal jet to pick up us at the Kennedy Airport. Our secret wish is about to come true. We wait at the airport with the British ambassador at our side. He gives us last-minute instructions on royal protocol. We burst with excitement and thrill at the prospect of attending the wedding. We feel special. Even before our actual meeting, we feel honored to be received by the queen. We are confident we are going to see the royal family. Why do we feel special, honored, accepted and so confident of attending the wedding? We believe the Queen of England has personally invited us to join her at her son's wedding. We base that belief on a bona fide invitation by the queen herself. We have reason to believe the invitation is authentic: the document is authoritative, the seal is genuine, and the queen's representative is by our side. We have a royal invitation accompanied by royal attention. A few days earlier we had only empty wishes; now we have every reason to believe we will attend. We are confident we'll attend the wedding because we believe the queen will keep her word. Our excitement and joy is based on all the reasons for believing we are going to the wedding. The reasons for our faith enable us to experience emotionally the longings we had.

Someone could have doubted our claim we were going to the royal wedding. But nothing could change the fact the queen had written the letter or the fact the British ambassador had made all the arrangements. Our faith would be secured with reasons—reasons that allow us to maintain our joy no matter what others thought. Our faith couldn't be shaken because we knew why we believed.

Do you want a confident assurance you will always be loved and be able to love? Know why you believe God will always love you. Do you want assurance you will always be accepted? Know why you believe God finds you acceptable. Do you want confidence you will always be secure? Know why you believe God will always fulfill His promises. Knowing why you believe is the secret to a fulfilled and joyful life. Knowing *why* you believe will enable you to lay claim to the love, acceptance, and security God already has for you.

But is it really that simple? Simple, yes. Easy? No. Life serves up many reasons to doubt that you're loved, accepted, and secure. Life with all its trials may bring you face to face with the stark reality that you are not loved by those around you. Can you still feel loved even during the tragedy of a lost love? You can if you know why you believe God loves you.

It's not too hard to feel accepted when friends are kind and loving. But what happens when you're falsely accused or unjustly mistreated? Can you still feel accepted when you're facing the cruel rejection of others? You can if you know why you believe God accepts you.

When all is calm and serene, it's not difficult to feel safe and secure. But when you fail a course in school, lose a job, face mounting debts or stand numbly gazing upon the lifeless body of a loved one—what then? Can you still have confidence, assurance and security when the walls of life come crashing in on you? You can if you know why you believe God is your security.

In fact, life with all its trials and difficulties is the very place God wishes to demonstrate His faithfulness to you. He wants you to know why you can believe Him to be your source of being loved, accepted, and secure. He wants to teach you how your faith can appropriate all the love, acceptance, and security you will ever need. Let's go on to learn how.

3

Trials—The Perfect Setting?

No two men could be more different than Peter and Paul in personality and style, yet they were unanimous on the value of trials: "I will rather boast about my weaknesses, . . . I am well content with weaknesses, with insults, with distresses, with persecutions, with difficulties, for Christ's sake . . ." (Paul, in 2 Cor. 12:9–10); "In this you greatly rejoice, even though now for a little while, if necessary, you have been distressed by various trials . . ." (Peter, in 1 Pet. 1:6).

Be content with mistreatment, persecution, and difficulties? Boast about personal weaknesses? Rejoice about trials? What possible value could these things have? Yet, Peter says,

> . . . who is there to harm you if you prove zealous for what is good? But even if you should suffer for the sake of righteousness, you are blessed. And do not fear their intimidation, and do not be troubled, but sanctify Christ as Lord in your hearts, always being ready to make a defense to every one who asks you to give an account for the hope that is in you, yet with gentleness and reverence (1 Pet. 3:13–15).

Peter shows the relationship between trials and accounting for hope, explaining to others why we trust Christ. He warns his readers that harsh persecution will soon envelop them (4:12), and instructs them to be prepared to face three challenges:

1. Expect to suffer for doing good.
2. Do not be afraid when your oppressors try to intimidate you.
3. Be ready to account for your hope.

Do you see it? When is the most likely time for you to be called upon to account for your hope? When things are great and you're sailing serenely down life's placid stream? Or when you're gutting it out, fighting for your life against the mad rush of life's experiences? It's obvious. We all learn best to account for our hope in the midst of trials.

One cannot see hope, just as one cannot see faith. Only the results of faith and hope (love, joy, peace, satisfaction, and contentment) can be seen in a person's life. Peter assumes that the kind of questions you will face as a believer are not "Why do you believe?" but rather "Why are you so joyful?" "Why do you have such a positive outlook?" "How can you feel so loved?"

As believers, our hope is in Christ who manages the affairs of our lives and who will bring all of history to a final consummation for His glory. We do not have to worry about how things will end because we know the outcome. Our lives can take on the characteristics of love, joy, peace, happiness and restfulness in contrast to the world's despair. When we know what we believe, then we can account for our hope by giving reasons why we believe in Christ.

The Christians to whom Peter wrote were living in a time of persecution just prior to Nero's reign. They faced growing hostility and no longer enjoyed the official sanction of the Roman authorities as a "sect" of Judaism. It had become clear that Christianity was distinct from the "approved" religion of the Jews. The Roman emperor had declared himself a god and the secular state of Rome was on an inevitable collision course with Christianity. Paul had probably made his formal defense before a Roman court, had been condemned, and now awaited martyrdom (2 Tim. 4:16–18).[1]

Peter's message is as relevant now as it was then: hope is best accounted for under fire. The only way to maintain a vibrant hope in God is to have faith tested—faith under fire gets proven results.

Trials, Not Temptations

A distinction must be made at the outset between trials and temptations. Trials test your convictions about God: who He is, what He can do, His wisdom and ability to meet your needs. Trials never test your morality, only your faith. Temptations, on the other hand, always have the sense of enticement to evil. God will test you but never tempt you. It would be contrary to His nature. God never lures you into sin.

James makes this point when he says:

Let no one say when he is tempted, "I am being tempted by God"; for God cannot be tempted by evil, and He Himself does not tempt any one. But each one is tempted when he is carried away and enticed by his own lust. Then when lust is conceived, it gives birth to sin; and when sin is accomplished, it brings forth death (James 1:13–15).

Temptation, the allurement away from God to sin, bites hard because of its ally within man: lust. Lust, in this context, a wrong desire, is the Trojan Horse that penetrates our strong defenses and destroys us from within.

Interestingly, the word James uses for *tempted* in 1:13 is the same word used in 1:3 ("the *testing* of your faith"). While the word is the same, the context clearly shows a complete difference in meaning. One means *test,* an ordeal of faith, and the other, *temptation,* a solicitation to evil. One examines our faith, the other excites our lust. God will never tempt you to sin; He will only test your faith.[2]

I believe trials come our way to develop at least two qualities: maturity and endurance.

DEVELOPING MATURITY

The continual exercise of faith stimulates growth; and trials give us the opportunity to exercise. Have you heard someone say, "Hey!

I don't need the hassles of trials"? But we do need it. The little phrase *if necessary* in 1 Peter 1:6 suggests there are special times when God knows that we *need* to go through trials. We do not always know what need is being met, but we can trust God to know and to do what is best. Trials are varied, and God matches the trial with our needs.[3] Trials provide the perfect setting in which our faith is exercised.

A mature person is one who can distinguish between good and bad choices. We mature most rapidly in those situations where discernment is required. As children grow they become increasingly more responsible and they learn how to handle themselves correctly in everyday situations. As time passes, they learn how to apply right principles to practical issues. Through practice and experience they learn how to make right choices.

The theme of maturity runs throughout the book of Hebrews like a silver strand and is captured in this one verse: "But solid food is for the mature, who because of practice have their senses trained to discern good and evil" (5:14). In his book *Three Steps Forward, Two Steps Back,* Chuck Swindoll writes concerning this verse:

> What is the sign of maturity? Practicing what you hear. Through practice you become mature. You see, it is one thing to grow *old* in the Lord, but is another thing to grow *up* in the Lord. . . .
> James [is] the New Testament's "Man from Missouri." He wants you to put to the test what you claim to believe—by doing it! A mature person is one who is involved in practicing on a regular, consistent basis what he hears and what he takes in. . . .
> When irritations come, obey God and carry out His Word in dealing with them. When temptations come, apply principles of Scripture that help you face them victoriously. When the sins of the flesh arise, apply the truths you have been taught. It is in the experience of all this application that you becomes wise and more mature.[4]

Trials present us with the opportunity to practice God's principles in our lives and to trust Him for the outcome. The growing up process involves being stretched . . . and pulled .   sometimes to the breaking point, but all the while committing ourselves, by faith, into the hands of the One who does all things well.

THE TESTING OF FAITH

I used to think that trials were necessary to develop character and to motivate me to be the kind of person God intended me to be. I thought God put me through the fires of testing to prove the purity of my character. It was like gold (doesn't the Bible use this illustration?): fire melts gold and burns out the impurities. Therefore, trials would purify my character and make me like Christ.

What a disappointment! It didn't work!

I flailed through one test after another and my character didn't improve. I just ground my teeth harder, trying to strain out patience, goodness, love and other qualities. I thought of trials as the spiritual barbells of life given to exercise my faith and develop strong spiritual physiques.

God doesn't put you in tests to reveal your weaknesses, or show you where you need to be strong. Trials are given for the purpose of testing your *faith*, an entirely different issue!

Now think this through with me. It may be a strange concept at first, but it will grow on you as we progress. Trials are a test of *faith*. James lays it out clearly when he says: "Consider it all joy, my brethren, when you encounter various trials, knowing that the *testing of your faith* produces endurance" (James 1:2–3, emphasis mine).

If trials tested character, and the secret to happy living was developed character, then bring on the trials! "Where are they Lord? Let me have more trials!" But the Word doesn't say you are matured by tested character, but by tested faith. Paul articulates this same principle when he shares that it is our faith that establishes us in our Christian walk. "As you have received Christ Jesus the Lord, so walk in Him, having been firmly rooted and now being built up in Him and *established [by]* your faith . . ." (Col. 2:6–

7). You enter the Christian life by faith *in Christ,* you walk by faith *in Christ* and you grow by faith *in Christ.* Everything you receive in the Christian life is from Christ by faith. That's why Paul says in another place that it is from "faith to faith" that you progress in the Christian life (Romans 1:17). Faith establishes, not tests.

When a trial confronts you—a death in the family, a financial reversal, a schedule delay—it is actually a test of your faith in God. God said He would comfort you (2 Cor. 1:3-4), lovingly provide all your needs (Phil. 4:19), and work things together for your good (Rom. 8:28). What, then, is being tested? Your character? Are you patient enough, content enough, secure enough? NO! *Your confidence that God will keep His Word is tested.*

This is the way faith is stabilized and matured: by the repeated experience of God fulfilling His Word when it appears He won't come through.

Peter also makes it clear that it is our faith which will be put to the test, not our character. Tested faith produces proven character, and in that order. The maturity of your faith depends on the *testing* of your faith. Your faith is tested, resulting in a renewed sense of courage, strength, and joy.

> In this you *greatly rejoice,* even though now for a little while, if necessary, you have been distressed by various trials, that the proof of your faith, being more precious than gold which is perishable, even though tested by fire, may be found to *result* in praise and glory and honor at the revelation of Jesus Christ; and though you have not seen Him, *you greatly rejoice with joy inexpressible and full of glory, obtaining as the outcome of your faith* the salvation of your souls (1 Pet. 1:6-9, emphasis mine).

Peter emphasizes the *result,* the *outcome* of your tested faith: "praise, glory and honor at the revelation of Jesus Christ" and "the salvation of your souls."

That "result" is found not only in a life hereafter, but in a life here and now. God's principles of life are given to describe the way you can obtain maximum joy in this life. The more you align your lifestyle with God's principles, to honor Him, the greater happiness and fulfillment you will experience. The outcome of the testing of your faith has immediate results here as well as an "eternal weight of glory" later (2 Cor. 4:17).

Both Peter and James raise our vision beyond the immediate horizon to the *product* of our tested faith. That is why you can *greatly rejoice* and *consider it all joy* when you encounter various trials. Your ability to rejoice hinges on your dependence on the Holy Spirit to help you comprehend *who* you are honoring and how *glorious* the final result will be.

I recently went through one of the darkest, most bewildering periods of my ministry. Through it I learned a helpful lesson in rejoicing in the *midst* of trials while focusing on the outcome of my test.

I was speaking at the University of Missouri when I came down with severe stomach cramps. The cramps continued until I couldn't stand up. I was rushed to the hospital where they diagnosed it as acute constipation. Upon my return home Dr. Richards checked me into the hospital for tests. He told me the results of the tests would be complete in a few days. The pain by that time had let up, so I resumed my travel.

The next day I flew to Seattle where I was to speak at the "Six Hours" Evidence for Faith conference. Dr. Richards phoned me at my motel room. "Josh, the tests show you have two large tumors blocking the valve opening at the top of your colon. We must operate immediately."

"I'm here over the weekend. Will Monday be soon enough?" I stalled.

"Monday's fine. I'll schedule surgery for 7:00 A.M." The line went dead. My stomach was queasy.

That night I walked alone down the streets of Seattle until 1:00 A.M. I couldn't sleep. A lot goes through your mind when you are facing surgery for tumors. I didn't tell any of my staff about the doctor's report. I didn't phone Dottie. I just continued to mull the possibilities over in my mind. "Why? What could all this possibly mean, Lord? I have a beautiful wife and three children that need me. I'm only forty-two. Is it cancer? Is it curable? Does this mean the end of my speaking ministry? Will I see my forty-third birthday?"

And then the verses in 1 Peter 1 and James 1 came to me: "Greatly rejoice, even though . . . distressed by various trials . . ."; "Consider it all joy . . . when you encounter various trials . . ." I had to think hard to cough up a reason to rejoice. My mind quickly leafed through my past. Have I been trusting the right person for the right reason during my life? If I had life to do over, would I entrust my life to my Lord and Savior Jesus Christ? Would I follow Him to marry the same woman, serve with the same people, do the same things and work with the same organization? I had to answer an emphatic "Yes!"

That night as I was still walking the quiet streets of Seattle my despair turned to joy. In tears, I told God that my decision to trust Him some twenty years ago had brought me maximum joy. I told Him my purpose in life was to bring Him praise, glory and honor. Whether He wanted me off the speaking circuit, in a hospital bed, or in heaven with Him, I wanted whatever brought Him the most honor. I began to thrill at the joy of my trial, knowing that its purpose was to glorify my Savior. Somehow He wanted to get honor out of my physical problem. I didn't know "why" at the time but I did know for what reason. I could rejoice at the thought of Christ being honored for what little I had to suffer.

I finished the conference, flew back home and checked into the hospital. After a few last-minute tests and an internal examination, Dr. Richards, along with some other specialists, said, "We can't understand this. Whatever was blocking your colon is gone. It may have been two large air bubbles. No surgery is necessary and you should be back to normal in a matter of days."

I don't know whether I ever had tumors or not. But one thing I do know: my moments of doubt gave me an opportunity to reaffirm my trust in Christ and to tell my wife, children, associates and doctors that I believed God knew what He was doing. Based on who I knew Christ to be, and what I knew the Bible to be, by faith I could commit my life, death, tumors, even air bubbles into His hands. There was reason to rejoice, not because my physical problem was resolved (and, believe me, that helped!), but because God was being seen as the master controller of my life and destiny.

Being able to rejoice during trials and pain might be called "training with a purpose." Have you ever wondered what motivates an athlete to tough it out through training camp, experiencing pain and grinding misery during practice? One track star told me, "Sure it hurts. Those last few meters are more painful than you can imagine. But I don't concentrate on the pain. If I did I could never win. I concentrate on winning!" We are not to focus on the pain of our trial, but rather the honor it brings to God.

The Apostle Paul said it forcibly and clearly: ". . . forgetting what lies behind, and reaching forward to what lies ahead, I press on toward the goal for the prize of the upward call of God in Christ Jesus" (Phil. 3:13–14).

DEVELOPING ENDURANCE

Consider it all joy, my brethren, when you *encounter various trials*, knowing that the testing of your faith produces *endurance*. And let *endurance have its perfect result*, that you may be perfect and complete, lacking in nothing (James 1:2–4, emphasis mine).

Endurance means to hold up under fire, to persevere through difficulties, to stick with it though the going is rough. Endurance causes us to stay committed to our convictions even when those convictions are tested and tried.

Trials have a special place in our lives as opportunities to develop endurance. You can endure "hardness as a good soldier" (1 Tim. 2:4), if you know your "commander" has your best interest at heart.

James uses a striking verb to describe the value of trials in our lives. He says, "Consider it all joy, my brethren, when you *encounter various trials*." To *encounter* is to confront something or someone face to face. In this case, you confront a choice. You must ask yourself: 1) will I continue to trust a loving God who cares about me and loves me and will meet all my needs at the best time; or 2) will I disregard God's guidelines and go out to secure illegitimately my needs in the way *I* think best?

The objective of the Christian life is to become men and women of enduring faith, following God's plan for maximum fulfillment and giving ultimate glory to God. Through repeated testings of your faith, you learn to believe God even in the face of contradictory circumstances.

My wife, Dottie, vividly remembers a trial she experienced several years ago. She was pregnant with our second child, Sean. Dottie had had mononucleosis three times and her body needed eight hours of sleep each night or a relapse could occur. To complicate matters, she would be traveling with me for two to three weeks per month after the baby came. Hopping from university to university with an infant and our two-year-old, Kelly, would require all the energy she could muster. My reassurances to help with both Kelly and the new baby were welcomed, but the closer the time came to have our child, the more Dottie prayed that God would provide her with a *sleeping* beauty.

Sean came, a bouncing, energetic, eight-pound four-ounce boy. A beauty he was; a sleeper he was not. Sean consistently woke up at least five to six times every night. One night, after a long and tiring day, Dottie shared with me her spiritual struggle. "Honey, I don't understand it. Why hasn't God answered my prayers? Doesn't God care if I get my rest or not? Is it selfish to want to be rested and healthy? This whole ordeal has become a test of my faith. Is God really faithful?"

Dottie could believe either that God knew what He was doing or that God really didn't care about her. It was her choice. Yet, she was reminded of the many instances in which God proved Himself to be faithful in her life and the lives of others in the past. Her faith was strengthened as she reaffirmed that she knew God knew what He was doing.

Night after night Dottie got less and less sleep. It was encouraging to watch her brief struggle with resentment undergo a transformation into praise for God's faithfulness and loving care. Her prayers became, "God, you know what is best for me. You know how much sleep I need. If you wish me to be tired for your glory, then let it be."

One night while Sean was awake crying, Dottie realized that God was being faithful to her and answering her prayer in an unexpected way by giving her supernatural strength. As she thought about it, in spite of the interruptions and lack of sleep each night, she was not overtired and could accomplish what she needed to do each day. When she understood this, her knowledge of God's faithfulness once again crystallized in her mind, and her faith was reinforced to trust such a dependable, loving God in other areas of her life. In the midst of a severe test of faith, Dottie was strengthened and God received the glory. And at fourteen months (to God's glory and Dottie's relief), Sean became the best sleeper of all our children.

Endurance, like maturity, chooses to wait for the best. It is willing to pass up temporary pleasures, momentary enticements, for the satisfaction of eternal, permanent glory. Endurance anticipates the outcome—and is willing to wait.

Moses made a choice to identify with God's cause rather than to enjoy sin's pleasure for a time. "By *faith* Moses, when he had grown up, refused to be called the son of Pharaoh's daughter; *choosing* rather to endure ill-treatment with the people of God, than to enjoy the passing pleasures of sin" (Heb. 11:24–25, emphasis mine).

There are a lot of passing enticements that look so satisfying. Satan specializes in masquerading pain as pleasure. He cloaks sin in a garment of innocence, hiding its bitter bite from the undiscerning eye. Yet, tests of faith are an opportunity to base our response on the knowledge that we serve a loving God who knows best what we need, when we need it.

Don't be mistaken. Sin does bring pleasure. So much pleasure, in fact, that people threaten their reputation, sacrifice their positions, even forsake what is dear to them, to experience it, to taste its flavor. But it is so temporary—now you see it, now you don't; and you do not remember what it was like, which is why you need more.

James announces that it is the work of endurance to hold you steady *now* in anticipation of the perfect *yet to come:* ". . . Let endurance have its *perfect result,* that you may be perfect and complete, lacking in nothing" (1:4).

Trials present you the opportunity to trust a loving, faithful God, to be content with His gifts, and to trust Him alone. When you do trust Him, endurance is the result.

An Opportunity to Know What and Why You Believe

When Jesus suffered the ordeal of His painful trial, crucifixion and death, He did so as an example for us to follow. Notice 1 Peter 2:21–23·

> For you have been called for this purpose, since Christ also suffered for you, leaving you an example for you to follow in His steps, who committed no sin, nor was any deceit found in His mouth; and while being reviled, He did not revile in return; while suffering, He uttered no threats, but *kept entrusting Himself to Him who judges righteously.*

Jesus had done no wrong; yet He was abused, mistreated, mocked, beaten, crucified and unjustly put to death. Christ did not deserve the treatment He received, but instead of fighting back (which He had the power to do), He submitted to the abuse of those who despised Him and loved them in return. How did Christ do that?

You might think that because He was the Son of God and had no sin, it was no problem for Him to be loving and kind in the face of injustice. Not so! Christ laid aside His prerogatives as God, was tempted in every point like ourselves, accepted abuse, and submitted to His Father's will to die on the cross for our sins (Phil. 2:5–8).

If Christ laid aside his *personal* right to justice, what enabled

Him to "utter no threats" and love His persecutors? Christ, our example, knew *in whom* He believed and *why* He believed Him. It was the *knowledge of why* He trusted His Father that resulted in perfect obedience. ". . . He uttered no threats, but kept *entrusting Himself to Him who judges righteously* . . ." (1 Pet. 2:23, emphasis mine).

His Father was the righteous judge. Christ could love His accusers because He believed His Father would demand justice. That belief relieved Christ from personally demanding justice Himself. His knowledge of His Father's character enabled Him to keep "entrusting Himself to Him who judges righteously."

Peter doesn't waste time in punching the point home. He looks you square in the eye a few pages later and says: "Therefore, let those also who suffer according to the will of God entrust their souls to a faithful creator in doing what is right" (1 Pet. 4:19). You can't escape his ironclad logic. The ultimate responsibility for setting everything right, extracting retribution and compensating for injustice in this life belongs to the Father Himself. When you suffer, you can trust God with your case because He does everything right.

Therefore, when you know the specific quality of God in which to trust (in this case, His faithfulness), that very reason for faith becomes the means God uses to provide the needed grace to endure hardship. When you know the reasons you can trust God, the *what* and *why* of your faith, you can feel loved and give love, even when the person you love betrays you. When you know the reasons that you are accepted by God, you can feel accepted even when you are rejected by others. When you know the reasons that you can be certain of the future, you can feel secure when life is coming apart at the seams.

God has a perfect timetable for meeting your needs. His jobs always get done. Trials test your belief in God's authority to control your circumstances, His wisdom to discern the best course, His power to accomplish His will, and His ability to arrange events for your good. Rejoice that God graces your life with trials. Your strengthened faith *can* result in the joy of knowing you are loved, accepted, and secure.

PART II

Means Being Loved

4

A Case Study in Lost Love

I strolled through the student union past the common TV parlor. The room was packed with every occupant intently absorbed in a program. I slipped inside to see what was of such interest.

"Believe me, Genesta, I love *you*—you've got to believe me." With head down, the actress softly asked, "But what about your wife?" The handsome doctor lifted Genesta's head tenderly and gazed passionately into her eyes. "Genesta, you are the only one who means anything to me any more. You've got to believe that."

A girl in the TV room broke the silence and absorption of the crowd as she blurted out: "If you believe him, Genesta, you're crazy." The crowd chuckled as the organ music swelled, the credits rolled, and the teaser for the next episode faded out.

That's par for the course for most daytime soap operas. But the TV dialogue reminded me once again of the relationship between faith and love: *"Believe* me, I love *you*—you've got to *believe* me." The fact is, your faith plays a more important role in your ability to love and be loved than you probably imagine. And the more you examine the nature of faith, the more you will see how love actually depends upon what you believe.

Many don't know of nor adequately comprehend the infinite love God has for them, and that God's love is eternal and unconditional. This thought has impressed me so lately that Dottie and I decided to use Christmas this year to remind ourselves, and our friends, of God's unconditional, unending love. To a number of our close friends and family members we sent a wooden framed plaque with this Scripture verse personalized to each family:

> Dear Dale and Brenda,
>
> Just as the Father
> has loved Me,
> I have also loved you;
> abide in My love.
>
> Jesus
> John 15:9

Then we enclosed this card that I wrote:

This verse truly describes the meaning of Christianity—in other words, that God has loved us and expressed that love through sending His Son Jesus Christ to die on the cross for our sins. And the challenge is to experience every day His love in our life and live in the reality that He unconditionally loves and accepts us.

That is indeed the challenge: to take what we know from God's Word of His eternal, boundless love and relate that to our minds, wills, and emotions by faith. And yet there are so many people who know God loves them, that His Son died for them, but for whom that realization has had little impact on their feelings of being loved. God's love is something they talk about, not something they experience in meeting practical needs.

A significant step in getting our love needs met and developing the freedom to return love is discovering the relationship between our faith in Christ and our need to love and be loved. There was a time, before coming to Christ, when I didn't see a relationship between faith and love. Tragically, even many *Christians* are blind to this truth. Faith for them becomes a part of a person's spiritual life exercised in prayer and worship and unconnected to loving and feeling loved; they separate faith from facts, practical matters from spiritual ones. Faith influences our communion with God—

it's only spiritual, they think. Loving and being loved affects our personal relationships—it's practical, unrelated to matters of faith. How wrong!

Faith was never meant to be merely a "spiritual" exercise that rarely touches our practical needs. Our love relationship with Christ is designed to teach every husband and wife, or parent and child, exciting insights for an abiding love for one another.[1] I see a definite and vital connection between faith in Christ and the ability to give and receive love. The challenge is to take what you know about God's love through faith and appropriate it in such a way that your emotions and those of the ones you love are transformed.

Let's look at the story of a real-life couple to see this process in action.

KAREN AND DAN

My wife and I greeted Karen warmly as she came off the plane. We had known Karen and her husband, Dan, for over eight years. We had lived near Karen and Dan in Dallas during my early ministry. Visiting together often, we soon became fast friends. Dan was from southern Missouri and Karen from Kansas. They had met as teenagers, and their friendship soon blossomed into romance, and romance into marriage. Dan worked long hours as a building contractor. They didn't have any children.

Now their marriage had run into trouble, and Karen had come for help. She said she had to get away and try to get her feelings sorted out. During the hour drive from the airport, Karen confessed her long, bitter story.

"All our married life I've had a hidden fear our marriage would break up," she said. "And now my nightmare has come true. It's not that I hate Dan for what's happened. I'm trying to forgive him. But I can't get over the feeling that Dan never did love me." Her head dropped. She broke into tears. "You know, you think you're close to someone; you think they really love you, and then you realize they don't love you. It's really painful. I know this other woman doesn't mean anything to Dan. He says he loves me, but right now, I don't know if I can ever love Dan, or any man, again."

Karen gave us a brief chronology of the breakdown of their relationship. The first crack appeared as a result of their social life. Their calendar, under Dan's command, was booked solid. Dan was a very likable person; he had a good sense of humor and knew how to make you laugh. And he genuinely enjoyed being with people. Karen wanted a more quiet life, though, time just to be together at home. But Dan insisted he needed the outside fellowship and friendship.

"It's gotten to the place I simply don't care if we go anywhere any more," Karen told us, riding back from the airport. "It wouldn't be so bad if I could just feel comfortable around his friends. But, honestly, I feel alone in those crowds. I'm always watching Dan talk to everyone else; he acts as though I don't exist. And the reasons why are pretty obvious when he focuses 90 percent of his attention on two or three women the entire evening."

"Did you talk to Dan about your feelings?" we asked.

"Yes," she said. "I talked to him and he said I was jealous. He said those girls meant nothing to him, and he was just being sociable."

Some months after their confrontation, as Karen recounted, another troubling sign appeared. Dan occasionally called one of the women of the church from work. They were on a church committee together and needed to discuss the details of a project, Dan explained. Karen accepted his explanation, but felt uneasy anyway. She felt such calls should be made from home.

The tension between Karen and Dan increased. At heart, Karen didn't trust Dan. And Dan resented Karen's attempts to restrict his freedom. Karen made it clear that if Dan really loved her, he would honor her feelings, not make secret phone calls, and cut back on his social life and the flirting that went with it. Dan made it equally clear that he thought Karen's jealousy was the real problem.

Then Dan's short affair happened.

As believers, Karen and Dan subscribed to the teachings of Christianity. Yet their faith, when Karen arrived to stay with us, was not helping them work out their problems. In fact, both of them used Bible passages to support their criticism of the other.

Through a series of conversations, with Karen directly and with Dan by phone, their separate perspectives on the problem, their emotional needs, and what each proposed as a solution became clear.

Karen's Perspective

"If Dan really loved me," she said, "he would cut down on all his party-going and devote more of his attention to me. When we go to a church function or an office party, he should treat me with more consideration than the other women there." Karen referred to 1 Peter 3:7: "You husbands likewise, live with your wives in an understanding way; . . . and grant her honor as a fellow heir of the grace of life. . . ." Karen remembered how Dan had longed to be with her every waking hour while they were dating. She found it impossible to understand why she couldn't fill Dan's need for friendship. She wanted to, badly.

Karen's Need

Karen needed to feel loved. She often said, "All I want is for Dan to *really* love me." She wanted more of Dan's attention as proof of his love for her.

Karen's "Solution"

Karen believed the fulfillment of her longing for love depended on her husband. She believed that if Dan would honor her according to God's Word (1 Pet. 3:7), the problem would be solved.

Dan's Perspective

Dan felt misunderstood and threatened. He thought it unfair to be accused of not loving his wife because he had other friends.

A wife, he thought, should not be contentious and jealous; she should submit to her husband's wishes, and, in this case, she should never have complained about Dan's social life. All of her haranguing had led to the affair; she had driven him into the other woman's arms.

Dan's Need

Dan needed to know he was loved. He wanted to feel appreciated and respected by others, as well as by his wife.

Dan's "Solution"

Dan believed his need for love and respect would be fulfilled by both his wife and friends. Dan was convinced that if Karen would understand his need to be appreciated, respected, and looked up to, as well as his need for additional friends, the problem would be solved.

Obviously, Karen and Dan had reached a point of stalemate. They both needed to know they were loved, but with the tensions that existed between them, how could they?

5

What Is Christianity?

Karen and Dan's faith was of little use in settling their differences because they had misconceptions about what "faith" is. If they had had even a limited understanding of the relationship of true faith to our need of loving and being loved, their problems might not have arisen. Or, even with the rupture having occurred, they could far more easily have understood the reasons for it and begun the rebuilding process. Let's digress now to examine closely how faith in Christ gives human relationships their distinctive shape; how His love can bring forth your love. Faith can transform all your relationships, but again, as with Karen and Dan, this cannot happen unless you understand it properly.

THE CENTRAL ISSUE: OUR RELATIONSHIP WITH CHRIST

One can hardly begin to discuss the core issues of the Gospel without immediately recognizing the relational aspects of Christianity. We have already seen that Christianity is fundamentally a faith relationship with a person—Jesus Christ—and that a Christian is one who has personally received Christ as Savior and Lord, thereby establishing a personal relationship with God by faith. All the other aspects of the Christian faith are built on that foundation. That's why in His public ministry Jesus always made His identity and our relationship with Him the crucial issue, so much so that His very methods of teaching refer back to His identity and our response to that disclosure. In His every gesture, remark, or sermon there is always the implicit question, "Who do you say that I am?" Our answer to that question decides what our relationship to Him will be, because in the act of recognizing Jesus as Lord we commit ourselves to Him. Thus, by insisting at every juncture on this question of His identity, Jesus makes our relationship to Him central. God's chief objective for Christ's coming and substitutionary death for us is to bring man and God together into a love relationship. That is why Christianity is first of all a relationship to Christ, *not* a religion or system of beliefs. We have abundant scriptural evidence for this.

Jesus' "I Am" Statements

Christ forced people to consider their relationship to Him by speaking of Himself in extraordinary ways. His famous "I am" statements illustrate how He made His identity central. For instance, Jesus said, "I am the bread of life," emphasizing that if anyone wanted to sustain his life, he must partake of Him (John 6:48). He said, "I am the door," and through their familiarity with sheep and shepherding, the Jews knew He meant the only way to safety and protection was through Him (John 10:9). He also said, "I am the vine, you are the branches," and the disciples knew He meant that spiritual life comes only from being related to Him as a branch is to a vine (John 15:5).

One of Jesus' most startling claims about Himself is in John 14:6, "I am the way, and the truth, and the life; no one comes to the Father, but through me." Jesus did not claim to know the way, He professed *to be* the way. He did not say He would teach the truth, but that He *was* the truth. He did not promise to explain the way to God; He *is* the way to God. People were forced in the presence of Jesus to make a decision about His identity and their relationship to Him. He did not allow any neutral ground.

Christianity Is Christ

I like to say that Christianity *is* Christ. Remove Christ from Christianity, and you have just an empty shell.

In contrast, most other religious leaders put their teachings out front and themselves in the background. Jesus put Himself ahead of His teachings. Others would say, "What do you think about what I said?" Jesus, again, asked, "Who do you say that I am?" The basis of most other faiths is a set of teachings; Christians, though, trust in Christ, not teachings. For example, if you remove Buddha from Buddhism, Buddhism still remains intact. Buddhism rests on Buddha's teaching that we must transcend this life and its inevitable suffering by ceasing to desire anything that fosters the "illusion" of personhood. The existence of Buddha, even before his death, was never the issue. The same is true of Confucius's importance to Confucianism, and Mohammed's importance to Islam.

But, if you remove the person of Christ from Christianity, there is no Christianity! Without the Person of Christ, Christianity crumbles. Why? Because Christianity is based on the person of Jesus Christ and our faith relationship with Him. Faith in Christ brings about a love relationship, whereas other religions bring an impersonal ideology to the forefront. Without Christ, Christianity would cease to exist, for it rests upon His identity as the eternal Son of God and our faith in Him as our personal Savior and Lord.

Often we erroneously focus on the *teachings* of Christ rather than the *Person* of Christ. Focusing on *teachings*, however, emphasizes adherence to impersonal rules, whereas directing one's faith to Christ emphasizes a personal relationship.

Now don't get me wrong. I think the doctrines of Christianity are important, but they rank second to our love relationship with Christ. It's that relationship that gives personal meaning to His teachings, for instance, His teaching on love.

A friend of mine, a talented, popular Christian recording artist, has been doing concerts for fifteen years. Recently Mark told me of his struggle as a young man because he didn't understand the relational aspect of his faith. Mark was raised in a Christian home, the son of a pastor. You might think that he would have learned sound doctrine and theology in that environment, and how Christ related to him. Unfortunately, this was not the case. His father, a strict disciplinarian, made sure he understood the rules of Christian living. Mark related, "I grew up believing that a Christian was a person who lived right and had his sins forgiven. I thought I stayed on good terms with God by following the rules. In my eyes, Christianity was merely a vast number of do's and don'ts, with no room for mistakes."

Every aspect of his life felt smothered by rules, Mark said, stifling his musical creativity. He became judgmental in spirit, alienated from people, even making deals with God. He assumed all Christians battled with these same feelings until he met a fellow musician, Bob, who shattered his conception of Christianity. Bob was content with himself as a person and didn't seem consumed with just following rules. Love and joy emanated from his life. When Mark learned that Bob accredited his joyful outlook on life to Christ, he was shocked and curious. Mark could hardly believe there was a dimension of his faith that he had missed.

Bob was influential in reforming Mark's concept of Christ. "Bob had a freedom, a contentment and peace I simply didn't have. Over a period of months Bob taught me what it really meant to be a child of God. He explained that his relationship with God was based on knowing a living Christ in the Scriptures, not *just* following rules. When I understood Christianity was faith in a person who loved me unconditionally I began to understand the meaning and purpose of obedience. I no longer obeyed God's law to prove my love, I obeyed *because of* my new love relationship with God. I realize now I never would have understood Christ's teachings until I understood my relationship with Christ."

Now Mark understands the difference between knowing Christ and simply following empty rules. Mark even lovingly explained to his parents how he felt, and they deeply regret that they did not express to him the relational truths about Christ.

The Gospel, the "Good News," tells how sinful man can have fellowship with a Holy God through faith in Jesus Christ, the one who died for our sins and rose from the dead. When anyone trusts in Christ, he enters into a right relationship with God. Christianity, then, is primarily God reaching down to us, offering us a relationship with Himself through Christ. Religion, by contrast, is man's attempt to reach God through good works and empty ritualizing, an attempt that always fails.

THE QUESTION OF JESUS' IDENTITY

We have seen that in Christianity the central issue is our relationship to Christ. It's critical, then, to ask, who is Jesus Christ? Is He worthy of my trust? Consider the implications: What if you place your faith in someone who is unable to fulfill your need for love? Wouldn't that make your faith hopeless and empty? After all, IF JESUS IS NOT GOD, THEN HE IS UNWORTHY OF YOUR FAITH AND UNABLE TO FULFILL YOUR NEEDS. You would then have no reason to seek a relationship with Him. So you need to know if Christ's claims to be God are valid.[1]

"I and the Father Are One"

Let's go to a major confrontation recorded in John's Gospel between Jesus and the Jews over His identity. During the Feast of the Dedication in Jerusalem, Jesus was approached by some Jewish leaders while He was at the temple. The Jews put it straight to Jesus, "How long will you keep us in suspense? If you are the Christ, tell us plainly" (John 10:24). Jesus' answer was as clear as crystal.

> Jesus answered them, "I told you, and you do not believe; the works that I do in My Father's name, these bear witness of Me. But you do not believe, because you are not of My sheep. My sheep hear My voice, and I know them, and they follow Me; and I give eternal life to them, and they shall never perish; and *no one shall snatch them*

out of My hand. My Father, who has given them to Me, is greater than all; and *no one is able to snatch them out of the Father's hand. I and the Father are one."* The Jews took up stones again to stone Him (John 10:25–31, emphasis mine).

One might wonder why there was such a strong reaction to Jesus' statement "I and the Father are one." There doesn't seem to be too much in it to get upset about. Some cults hold that Jesus simply meant He was one with the Father in purpose, desire, or goal. They would say that Jesus affirmed nothing more than His dedication to do the will of the Father. That sounds plausible enough until you look at *how* Jesus said, "I and the Father are one." An interesting feature of this phrase arises when the Greek is studied. A. T. Robertson writes that *one* is neuter, not masculine, in the New Testament Greek, and does not mean one in purpose, but rather, one in "essence or nature."[2] Jesus said in effect, "I and the Father are one in essence and nature, character and substance as God." Whatever God is, Jesus is.

Now see how the people He spoke to understood him. "The Jews took up stones again to stone Him. Jesus answered them, 'I showed you many good works in the Father, for which of them are you stoning Me?' The Jews answered Him, 'For a good work we do not stone You, but for blasphemy; . . . because You, being a man, make Yourself out to be God' " (John 10:33).

It could not be more evident that the Jews understood that Jesus was claiming to be God. Their actions show this: the Old Testament named only a handful of crimes that demanded the capital punishment of stoning, blasphemy being one of them (Lev. 24:16).

But there's a dimension to Jesus' claim we haven't examined yet, which shouldn't be missed. Jesus equates His actions with those of the Father, in this case the action of holding souls in His hand. To be in His hand is to be in intimate, personal relationship with both the Father and the Son. Note the parallel between John 10:28 and 29.

"I give eternal life to them; . . . no one shall snatch them out of My hand.

"My Father . . . has given them to Me; . . . no one is able to snatch them out of the Father's hand."

Why can't they be snatched from Christ's hand? Because His hand, and the Father's hand, are the same hand! "I and the Father are one."

Jesus' Power to Forgive Sins

Mark 2:3–12 records another instance in which Jesus boldly claimed to be God. Friends brought a paralytic to Jesus while He was speaking in a private home. Unable to get through the door because of the crowd, they went up on the flat roof, removed the tiling, and let the man down with ropes in front of Jesus.

And Jesus seeing their faith said to the paralytic, "My son, your sins are forgiven." But there were some of the scribes sitting there and reasoning in their hearts. "Why does this man speak that way? He is blaspheming; who can forgive sin but God alone?" (Mark 2:5–7).

Someone might say, "Big deal! I can forgive sin. Somebody may sin against me, and I can say, 'I forgive you.' And he's forgiven. Does that mean I'm God?" No.

Yes, you and I can forgive sin when somebody sins against us. We can say, "You're forgiven," and they're forgiven. But that's not what Jesus did here.

The Jews quoted Isaiah 43:25 to back up their contention that only God could ultimately forgive sin. When Jesus said, "My son, your sins are forgiven," He was claiming to be God, because Isaiah didn't mean sin that you and I commit against each other; he meant sin committed against God. And only God can forgive sin committed against God. Jesus agreed fully. That's why He said, "I forgive you." Whew! No wonder they got upset.

But Jesus went a step further. How could Jesus possibly certify that He had the power to forgive this man's sins? The Jews couldn't see what took place in heaven. How could they know that Jesus wasn't a fake?

"But in order that you may know that the Son of Man has authority on earth to forgive sins," He said to the paralytic, "I say to you, rise, take up your pallet and go home" (Mark 2:10–11).

Jesus certified the transaction that could not be seen (forgiving the man's sin) by what could be seen (healing the sick man).

This object lesson in Christ's power to heal and forgive sin was not to emphasize His teachings, but His identity. He wasn't interested in discussing the latest rabbinic theory on bodily healing. Nor was he wanting to set out ten steps to follow for healing paralytics. Not that Jesus' teachings were unimportant; but if He is not *the* truth, then all His statements and parables are nice museum pieces, and His promises must go unfulfilled. Today as well, Jesus forces us to consider that it's our love relationship with Him that meets needs, not simply following a system of beliefs.

Jesus as the Authority for His Own Teaching

The validity, authority, and truthfulness of all that Jesus taught depends on His identity as God. Here the emphasis on Christ's identity as God unites with the importance of Christian doctrine; because the doctrines of Christianity are generated by who Jesus is. If Jesus wasn't God, our faith in Him would be meaningless and we'd have no doctrine to teach.

The Sermon on the Mount demonstrates this. The common people marveled at the authority of Jesus' words, noting the crucial difference between His teachings and those of the rabbis of His day (Matt. 7:28–29). These earthly teachers appealed to higher authorities than themselves. Jesus didn't. Repeatedly Jesus said, "You have heard it said of old . . . but *I* say unto you. . . ." He appealed only to Himself. *Who* He was made *what* He said important. His teachings are self-reflective to the point that His identity becomes the central issue, circling us back to the question of our relationship to Him. Christ Himself is both the content of and authority for His own teaching.

Jesus' Authority Confirmed by His Trial

Jesus' appeal to Himself as the authority of His teaching is further confirmed by His trial. Most people are tried in a court of law for what they have allegedly done. Christ was tried for who He was.

Remember the Jewish leaders' response to Pilate's questions? Pilate asked them, "Why do you want to put Him to death?" And they cried out, "Because He, being a man, makes Himself out to be God."

Look at the proceedings of the trial in Mark 14.

And the high priest arose and came forward and questioned Jesus, saying, "Do you make no answer to what these men are testifying against you?" But He kept silent, and made no answer. Again the high priest was questioning Him, and saying to Him, "Are you the Christ, the Son of the Blessed One?" (Mark 14:60–61).

Given the Jewish frame of reference at that time, when the high priest said "Son of the Blessed One," he referred directly to God. The high priest wanted Jesus to commit Himself. So he asked point-blank, "Are you God?" Until this point in the trial, Jesus had not spoken but just listened to the false witnesses, even though He had the right to question His accusers. But now He answered the high priest. Why did He choose to speak just then?

In Matthew 26:60–66 we have more detail about the trial of Christ. Matthew shows that at this point in the proceedings the high priest put Jesus under oath and He had to answer. The high priest said, "I adjure You by the living God, that You tell us whether You are the Christ, the Son of God" (Matt. 26:63). Christ was obligated now to answer.

" . . . I am; you shall see the Son of Man sitting at the Right Hand of Power. And coming with the clouds of heaven." And tearing his clothes the high priest said, "What further need do we have of witnesses? You have heard the blasphemy; how does it seem to you?" And they all condemned Him to be deserving of death (Mark 14:62–64).

Usually, when the Sanhedrin, the Jewish Supreme Court, met to hear a case, they would retire from the chamber and return, bringing in their verdict, much like modern-day juries. It was standard practice that after they had delivered their verdict, the high priest would reach down and make a very small tear at the hem of the garment he was wearing. The tear, approximately one-half inch in length, symbolized the conclusiveness of the verdict. His action was analogous to one of our judges bringing down his gavel.

A provision was made, however, for the high priest to tear his garment *before* the verdict was brought in. He was to do so in the presence of blasphemy—in this case, the offense of claiming to be God. Thus, the chronology of Mark 14:63–64, the exact sequence of events, testifies that Christ claimed before these magistrates to be God. "And tearing his clothes the high priest said, 'What further need do we have of witnesses? Behold, you have heard the blasphemy. How does it seem to you?' And they all condemned Him to be deserving of death." Note that the penalty was pronounced *after* the high priest tore his garments. This reversal of the usual sequence reaffirms that the central issue at the trial was Jesus' claim to be God.

The Jewish court found nothing offensive about Jesus' teaching, only that He appealed to His identity as God to validate what He said. The teachings of Christ lose their purpose if Christ is not God, for then He becomes just another voice among the din of world religious leaders. Every law and every tenet of Christendom hinges on Christ's identity as God. Without Christ being God, the teachings of Christianity are nothing but a lifeless set of rules.

Lightless Light

Christmas is a special time of year for our family, and we make a big deal of putting up the Christmas tree. I remember an interesting discussion that was brought about one year by our problems with the lights.

Do you remember those tree lights wired in a series in which one faulty bulb keeps the whole string from working? They are exasperating! We had replaced those sets, I thought, but on this particular Christmas I got hold of one of the old "series" sets that hadn't been thrown away. Of course, when I plugged it in, the set didn't go on. I jiggled and twisted the plug, thinking I had a bad connection. Finally I called to my wife, "What's wrong with these Christmas lights? They won't light."

I've thought of that a number of times since. They really weren't Christmas *lights*. I'd referred to a string of Christmas *bulbs* as lights, but they're not really "lights." Until they are lit, they are only useless bulbs—a darkened shell for the light to shine in. They are "lightless" lights.

How true that is of Christianity. We may call the teachings of Christ "Christianity," but if the person of Christ is not central, the teachings are an empty, darkened shell. Christ's teachings are meaningless or void without Him; as meaningless as a bulb that will not light. If it were not for Christ's incandescent presence shining through our lives by the Holy Spirit, Christianity would be just a dark set of rules, dim adornments against the darkness of life.

Rules *alone* cannot, properly speaking, be called Christianity at all. Yet they have a purpose. Let's move on to see how the teachings of the Bible, sometimes termed "the law," are also designed to bring us into a love relationship with Christ.

6

The Law and God's Character

I like to teach my three children—Kelly, Sean, and Katie—right
and wrong by teaching them about God. Teaching them standards
of moral behavior, even guidelines for healthy love relationships,
by pointing to God's character can be quite a challenge. So many
parents give their children reasons for their views of right and
wrong by saying, "Because I said so, that's why!" or even, "Because
that's what the Bible says." But I like to say, "Because God is
like that."

When I come home after a trip, to give my wife a break, I'll
take the kids out to breakfast. While in the car driving to the
restaurant or while eating, I'll suggest a particular moral situation
in which we'd be called upon to make an ethical decision. The
four of us will discuss it, and try to decide what course of action
to take, based on God's law. First we have to determine what
law or commandment applies, but the important thing then is to
see how that law originates and grows out of God's character; how
it reflects God's love for us and His desire for us to act in a way
that will result in our becoming all he has in mind for us. My
purpose is to acquaint my children with the kind of God we serve,
not just the kind of laws we follow.

THE CASE OF THE "FREE" COKE

My seven-year-old son, Sean, and I stopped at the local Chevron station for gas, and he dashed to the cold drink machine for a Coke. To his surprise, he not only got his Coke, but his money back. Elated with this stroke of fortune, he excitedly told me what had happened. After listening for a few moments, I interjected, "Sean, who do you think that money really belongs to—you or the station owners?" He looked at his Coke, to the money in his hand, and back to his drink. Nodding his head slightly, he admitted, "I guess the money belongs to those people in there," pointing to the attendant. He quickly returned the money.

As we drove away, I questioned him. "Sean, if we knew that money belonged to those people, would it be right to keep it?"

"No, Dad, that wouldn't be right."

"Why?" I probed.

It didn't take him long to answer. "It would be stealing."

I continued, "Why shouldn't we steal?"

He responded, "The Bible says we shouldn't steal."

"That's right, son." I replied, but then added, "Why does the Bible say we shouldn't steal?"

That stumped him. He thought awhile. Then, self-confidently, he said, "Because stealing is selfish and God said it was wrong."

"That's good, Sean. Stealing comes from a selfish attitude; God says selfish attitudes are wrong, so stealing is wrong." Sean sat back relieved. He had solved the puzzle.

I didn't want to discourage him, so I waited for a few minutes. "You know Sean, God doesn't want us to steal or be selfish. And you *weren't* selfish, because you took the money back. But there's a reason God doesn't like 'selfish' stealing. Do you know what that is?"

Sean didn't know.

"There is something about God's nature," I continued, "the way He is, that doesn't like stealing."

Now we were circling back to the source of things. "You see,

Sean," I explained, "God is fair and He wants Kelly and Katie to be fair to you and He wants you to be fair to them. So one of the ways He teaches us fairness is to say, 'Don't steal.' God loves us and He knows we are happier when people are fair with each other."

My son began to understand both the character of God and the importance of our relationship with Him.

Soon after the Coke machine episode, Sean traveled with me to a speaking engagement in Austin, Texas. I was to speak to a group of lawyers on the erosion of religious liberties in American society today. I was nervous. I wanted this talk to make the right kind of impression on the attorneys. I began my talk.

Midway through my address, Sean burst open a side door and blurted out, "Hey, Dad—guess what! I got a Coke out of the machine and the money came back too. Ain't that neat?"

He popped out of the room. That was it!

I was horrified. Oh no! I thought. All of my teaching down the drain. And these lawyers will think I'm raising a criminal son. My mind raced, "What will I say?" All the attorneys laughed and joked about his good fortune.

I tried to explain how I taught my children right and wrong behavior by relating their actions back to the character of God and how apparently Sean had missed the point of my teaching. However, at that very moment, Sean popped his head into the room.

"Oh, by the way, Dad," he enthusiastically proclaimed, "don't worry; I took the money to the front desk."

Whew! My sigh of relief reached all the way to the back of the room.

This outlook applies to other ethical issues as well. Lying is wrong because God is a God of truth. Cheating is wrong because God is just. Hatred is wrong because God is love. All these things are wrong because they are contrary to the very nature of God.

God's laws or commands are not an independent standard, set apart, by itself establishing a code of conduct. God's laws are an expression of His character, His nature. God's laws are to be obeyed, then, because they come directly from what God is like. That helps us to know Him better. His laws become pathways constructed not only to lead us to a knowledge of God but also to give us a guide by which to live.

There is an important, and often misunderstood, relationship between God and God's law. And a right concept of how God's laws reflect God's character is an important key to unlocking the secrets of both loving and being loved. In order to know how the law operates in our relationship to Christ, we need to study its various layers. The law still reveals the character of God to us today, shows us our need of His love, and points to the way in which we can reciprocate that love. It does so with a three-step plan, a divinely ordained progression characterized by clearly expressed *precepts* and universal *principles* that lead to the *Person* of God Himself.

THE LAW AS PRECEPT

This is the most common representation of the law—all those rules, regulations, codes, and requirements. Not surprisingly, because we are so achievement-oriented, this is the level where most of us start in our understanding of God's law. And unfortunately, most of us stop here, too.

Yet it's no surprise that God reveals Himself to us in this way, with precepts. Most of us understand specific commands, and God must speak to us where we are.

Precepts function with a two-pronged purpose: to contrast our way with God's way; and to reveal the solution to our alienated condition.

The Law Points Out Our Wrong

Because all of God's precepts are true, everything unaligned with them is false. That helps me understand that God's character, as revealed in God's Word, is the final authority for ethics. The law contrasts God's way with my human way, and in so doing rebukes anything in my life inconsistent with His standards.

The word "law" is often used to mean all of God's standards of righteousness. Through the law (precepts) God makes clear the requirements for fellowship with a holy God. Think back to when God gave His moral standards at Mount Sinai. Lightning, fire, thunder, smoke, and trumpet blasts filled those days. These phenomena were signs of God's greatness (Exod. 19:16). When the Israelites got close to their Lord they saw how unlike Him they were.

The Apostle Paul refers to this regulative aspect of the law in his classical theological treatise, the Book of Romans. He shows how the law makes us accountable to God.

> Now we know that whatever the Law says, it speaks to those who are under the Law, that every mouth may be closed, and all the world may become accountable to God; because by the works of the law no flesh will be justified in His sight; for through the Law comes the knowledge of sin (3:19–20).

The law is an excellent critic. It awakens a man's conscience. It pulls back the curtains, raises the shades, and opens windows to let the light of God's holiness flood the shadowy, dust-laden, and disheveled abodes of our souls.

An enlightened conscience will either excuse itself or try to live up to the new standard that's been set. Because of God's absolute standard of perfection, however, our best efforts will only increase our sense of sinfulness. The law cannot save; it only condemns (Gal. 2:16). But after understanding our plight, we are convinced that a merciful God must have provided another way for us to be reconciled with Him.

The Law Points Us to Christ

While the law can't change us (Romans 7 and 8 show us it's powerless to do so), it not only urges us to seek another means of reconciliation but guides us further in finding the solution to our sinfulness.

In fact, the Bible tells us that the law leads us by the hand, like a child going to school, to learn the lesson of faith: "Therefore the law has become our tutor [literally, child-conductor] to lead us to Christ, that we may be justified by faith" (Gal. 3:24). In the Greek-speaking world of Paul's day, there was a type of household servant called the *paidagogos*. He was in charge of the child's moral welfare, and it was his duty to oversee the child's character development as he became a man. One of his essential responsibilities was to take the child to school each day. He was not the child's teacher, but he was responsible to see that the child was, in fact, under the teacher's care. Paul borrows this picture from the culture of his day, and says, in effect, that the law has this same function. The law leads us to Christ, the Master Teacher, the only one able to show us how to establish a relationship with God.[1]

THE LAW AS PRINCIPLE

There is a second tier in this progression of God's self-revelation through the law. Since all of God's laws are pathways constructed for the purpose of knowing Him, principles are the intermediate step on the stairway leading us from precepts to the person of God. Behind each specific command (precept) there is a principle. A principle is a norm or standard that may be applied to more than one type of situation. To help explain the difference between a principle and a precept, think of a principle as expressing the fundamental truth on which a precept is based. You've probably asked "why" a hundred times or more whenever particular laws were laid down to you. Remember, principles help explain "why" by giving the reason behind the command. For example, there are a number of specific teachings in the Bible concerning sexual purity: "You shall not commit adultery" (Exod. 20:14); "Everyone who looks on a woman to lust for her has committed adultery with her already in his heart" (Matt. 5:28). The principle behind these related commandments is sexual purity. Yet, no doubt, behind that is another principle, that of faithfulness in marriage, and behind that principle is the character of God's abiding, unconditional love.[2]

God is pleased for us to know why we follow certain commands. That knowledge gives us a basis for our belief and solidifies obedience as a pattern of life. God wants us to obey the law for the right reason—to know Him—not out of mindless habit.

Principles also unmask our intentions, revealing the true motive of our hearts. For instance, in Jesus' admonition on adultery, which is based on marital faithfulness, He goes straight to the essence of the problem by showing that an attitude of lustfulness precedes any physical act. In fact, Christ shows us that our attitude is the basis on which He judges us, not on our success in our skulduggery (Matt. 5:28). Thus, principles do not dictate what your actions should be in specific situations as much as identify motives behind actions, as well as discerning their worth. They force you to consider why you're doing what you're doing.

So principles, even more than precepts, bring into focus your relationship with God. If you truly love God and want to glorify Him, you'll make decisions based on a desire to honor His principles of life. To live by principle is to live by love.

If you obey God's law out of any other motivation than to glorify Christ, you are in danger of practicing legalism. Keeping commandments must not become an end in itself. Legalism is interested only in keeping the rules; it is not concerned with the larger issue, our relationship with God. In fact, legalism can be a means of avoiding a love relationship with God.

Isaiah had something to say about those who followed the letter of the law without focusing on the person of God.

Because this people approach me with their mouths and honour me with their lips while their hearts are far from me, and their religion is but a precept of men, learnt by rote, therefore I will yet again shock this people, adding shock to shock: the wisdom of their wise men shall vanish and the discernment of the discerning shall be lost (Isa. 29:13–14).

"By rote" means mechanically, simply obeying because it's expected. The prophet tells us clearly that God has nothing but contempt for such obedience.

Faithfulness is not produced by mechanical performance of the law. It is a love relationship with a faithful God that produces faithfulness. Legalism can be defined as motivation by intimidation. Freedom from the bondage of the law, on the other hand, is obedience to Christ based on a motivation to please *Him*—in a word, love.

One modern prophet who has analyzed the contemporary church accurately and with wonderful insight is Charles Colson. A former Watergate conspirator and Special Counsel to former President Nixon, Mr. Colson met Christ personally in 1974 and has become a clarion voice calling Christians back to holy living through serious Christian commitment. He remarks concerning holiness and the danger of legalism:

. . . Seeing holiness only as rule-keeping breeds serious problems: first, it limits the scope of true biblical holiness, which must affect every aspect of our lives. Second, even though the rules may be biblically based, we often end up obeying the rules rather than obeying God; concern with the letter of the law can cause us to lose its spirit. Third, emphasis on rule-keeping deludes us into thinking *we* can be holy through our efforts. But there can be no holiness apart from the work of the Holy Spirit—in quickening us through the conviction of sin and bringing us by grace to Christ, and in sanctifying us—for it is grace that causes us to even *want* to be holy. And finally, our pious efforts can become ego-gratifying, as if holy living were some kind of spiritual beauty contest. Such self-centered spirituality in turn leads to self-righteousness—the very opposite of the selflessness of true holiness.

. . . Holiness is much more than a set of rules against sin. Holiness must be seen as the opposite of sin. . . . Conforming to the character of God—separating ourselves from sin and cleaving to Him—is the *essence* of biblical holiness, and it is the foundational covenant, a central theme running throughout Scripture.[3]

God desires that obedience to the law be a result of a love relationship, not as a basis to produce one. God does not want mere performance. Duty produces obligation, not joyful obedience. God gave His law to prescribe the way for a personal love relationship with Him. Obedience and right living become a natural by-product of that love relationship.

Have you discovered that requiring obedience to rules, without the context of a relationship, produces rebellion? But on the other hand, rules within this context create an atmosphere of loving response.

Picture this idea as two equations:

$$\text{Rules} - \text{Relationship} = \text{Rebellion}$$

$$\text{Rules} + \text{Relationship} = \text{Response}$$

Biblically, this is how you get to know the One in whom you believe. Unless you know the character of the person with whom you are having this relationship (God), you can't respond appropriately to the rules. But with a relationship, the rules take on significance. If you want to remove the drudgery from obedience, fall in love with Jesus. Being obedient should be a *result* of our love for Christ. Applying the principles on which specific commands are built is a kind of litmus test of all this. It exposes your essential motivation: either fear or love.

The Apostle Paul, in speaking to our motivation for obeying God's law, summed it up perfectly: ". . . love therefore is the fulfillment of the law" (Rom. 13:10). You see, God is love. And because He manifested that love in Christ, *because He first loved us in the gift of Christ as the fulfillment of the law,* we may reciprocate His love in obeying His law.

Picture the law like this:

```
                                              Character of God
                                          _____
                                          Reflected in Principles
                                              and Precepts



                              Eternal Principles
                          _____
                          Reflect God's
                          Character




        Specific Precepts
    _____
    Practically Apply
    Principles
```

Understanding the character of God is essential to understanding the law. For the character of God has not changed, nor has His expectation of holiness, faithfulness, and love from His people.

THE PERSON BEHIND THE LAW

To know what we believe about God's precepts and even God's principles and not know the character of God from which they derive is valueless. Too many times we focus on His *law*, and never see its extensions, what it teaches us about the character of God and His desire to love us personally.

Moses, who received the law for Israel, understood God's desire for a personal relationship with us better than anyone in the Old Testament. Exodus 33:11 says God spoke to Moses "face to face, as a man speaks with his friend." Later, in the same chapter, Moses prays to know God's ways: "Now therefore, I pray Thee, if I have found favor in Thy sight, let me know Thy ways, *that I may know Thee* . . ." (Exod. 33:13, my emphasis). You see, Moses longed to know God's ways, His precepts and principles, in order to be in fellowship with God.

The Bible reveals God. It tells what God is like. Words like *holiness, faithfulness,* and *love* are frequent Bible terms that describe God, but are hard to visualize. So God taught His people (and us) the meaning of these qualities by legislating many external ceremonies and requirements for Israel. The ceremonies were important, not in themselves, but in how they modeled holiness, faithfulness, and love. Each was an object lesson visualizing separation *from* defilement and sin, and separation *to* God. Israel would never have understood these terms had they not been illustrated in familiar, everyday terms.

When Israel was told, "Thou shalt have no other gods before Me," God wanted them to separate themselves from unholy practices to be preserved for fellowship with God alone. What is the principle behind this command? It came from the very character and nature of God Himself. Throughout the book of Leviticus we continually find such verses as this: "Thus you are to be holy to Me, for I the Lord am holy; and I have set you apart from the people to be Mine" (20:26). In fact, God issued very specific civil and ceremonial laws for Israel to reinforce this concept of being "set apart."

Many are tempted to skip over these chapters in Exodus and Leviticus that describe in detail the regulations concerning dress, food preparation and consumption, construction of the tabernacle, the forms of worship and the like. Altars and acacia wood and cubits and blended fabrics sound irrelevant today, superseded by the atonement of Christ. But this is a perfect example of the necessity of understanding God's laws in the light of God's character. Such prescriptions, instructions, and civil codes reveal the very character of God Himself. The purpose of these laws was to give Israel an object lesson in purity, separating good from bad, clean from unclean. The principle behind the law—purity of life—was based on the character and nature of God Himself. Specific laws prohibiting mixing threads in the same garment or hitching different types of animals to the same yoke were tangible lessons in the very character of God. He wanted His people to understand what He was like, that He was a God who did not tolerate sin. Their obedience to these laws was to point them to the perfect model of God's holiness.[4]

The law is not an end in itself. The law is based on principles that are the expression of God's character. The law is a means of knowing the person behind the law. The purpose of the law, then, is to draw us into personal acquaintance with the lawgiver.

The Psalms abound with praise to God, and in so doing they specify attributes of His character. Psalm 19 praises God for who He is by enumerating qualities of His law.

> The law of the Lord is *perfect,* restoring the soul; The testimony of the Lord is *sure,* making wise the simple. The precepts of the Lord are *right,* rejoicing the heart; The commandment of the Lord is *pure,* enlightening the eyes. The fear of the Lord is *clean,* enduring forever; The judgements of the Lord are *true;* they are righteous altogether.

Look at each quality in order:

1. __Perfect__   4. __Pure__

2. __Sure__   5. __Clean__

3. __Right__   6. __True__

Why do you think the law possesses these qualities? Yes, it's because they are also descriptive of God's character. Notice David describes the law of the *Lord.* The law, apart from God, is not perfect, sure, right, pure, etc. It is the law *of the Lord* that is perfect, sure, right, pure, clean, and true. God's law reveals God's true character.

7

The Law and God's Motivation

C. S. Lewis reports that a schoolboy was once asked what he thought God was like. He replied, "The sort of person who is always snooping around to see if anyone is enjoying himself and then trying to stop it."[1]

I'm afraid that's the sort of idea in many Christians' minds whenever God's law is discussed: God's law interferes with your freedom and keeps you from having a good time.

We've just discussed the idea that the role of God's law in a Christian's life is to reveal God's character. Some speak as if the "angry Jehovah" of the Old Testament and God as we see Him in Christ were two entirely different beings. But "God is love" applies to both the Old and New Testaments, and thus God's law, as an expression of His character, is also an expression of love. The realization that God has our good in mind in setting down laws will give us a whole new perspective for getting to know the kind of God we serve. God doesn't issue commands to cramp our lifestyle and limit our liberty. Instead, His law defines the limits in which our liberty can be fully expressed.

The Old Testament writers understood God's motivation in setting down His law. Deuteronomy emphasizes this:

"And now, Israel, what does the Lord your God require from you, but to fear the Lord your God, to walk in all His ways and love Him, and to serve the Lord your God with all your heart and with all your soul, and to keep the Lord's commandments and His statutes *which I am commanding you today for your good?"* (10:12–13, my emphasis).

Moses articulates here God's motivation for giving Israel the law: *for your good.* This same point is scattered throughout Deuteronomy (cf. 5:29; 6:18; 8:18; 30:15–20).

I live in southern California, and to drive on the freeways there is the experience of a lifetime. Even with the traffic laws, there are times you have to literally drive for your life! The laws define the way the traffic moves: when you must stop, how you may turn, how fast you may travel. All those regulations are for the good of the motorist, to insure his safety and provide good driving conditions. I don't chafe under the law that says you must drive on the righthand side of the road. That regulation defines a pattern for safe driving.

We need to understand God's law in the same way. Acknowledge that God knows best and that He knows just what you need for happy, fulfilled living. So obey His commands, not out of the fear of getting zapped if you don't, but in the knowledge that His law expresses God's best for you. We are created by divine design to function best within the context of God's laws. If we disregard God's laws in sin, we crash—and suffer the consequences.

In fact when God issues a negative command there are always two positive motives behind it: one, to protect you and the other to provide for you.

THE DANGER FROM OURSELVES

God desires to protect us from the harm of our ill-informed choices. He gives us His law so that we won't try and meet our own needs and miserably fail—and suffer the consequences! He loves us so much that He wants to protect us from the pain that will surely result from pursuing our own choices. His law maps out His step-by-step plan for doing just that.

Sin always brings destruction: spiritually, mentally, and physically.

He gives His law, then, to guide us away from those choices that would bring us pain. As a child of God I want to live compatibly with His nature, and His law gives me those guidelines. The law identifies many wrong choices that might otherwise look harmless.

FINDING REAL HAPPINESS

Also, if God is love (and He is), and if you're His dear child, then the law defines how a loving God has chosen to provide for you. When God says, "Don't," you know He has other, even better, provisions to give you if you will obey Him.

It's in this context that the Psalm writer claims, "No good thing does He withhold from those who walk uprightly" (Ps. 84:11). Also, "They who seek the Lord shall not be in want of any good thing" (Ps. 34:10). God wants to meet your needs. He's able to do anything. Yet, if He's withholding something from you, by virtue of issuing a command against it, you can rest assured it's because He has something better in store for you later.

I understood this when I broke up with a girl I was engaged to. I loved her and thought she was everything I ever wanted in a wife. Yet God wouldn't give us peace about our relationship. And it hurt to break off that relationship. I remember when my plane rolled away from the gate where I had left her, having seen her for possibly the last time, I thought my heart would break. I was angry at God. I wanted to run off that plane and shout, "I love you! Let's get married."

Yet I knew that was wrong. As the plane taxied to the runway, I prayed, angrily. "God, how can you be so unloving, so uncaring?"

"Josh," God seemed to say, "I will withhold no good thing . . ."

"Is this a 'good thing'? It hurts!"

"I will withhold no good thing. . . ."

"But what about *her?* She's the best thing that ever happened to me!"

And then it seemed I understood, "Then . . . the woman you will give me will be better than her?" No, that didn't seem right.

"Not necessarily better than Paula," God seemed to say, "but better for *you* than Paula. I'm not punishing you. I only want the best for you."

Because I serve a God who loves me and provides for me, and has proven that in the past, in my life and in the lives of others, I was able to accept momentary heartache in anticipation of the greater good God was bringing to me. The struggle was made easier because I knew why he directed me to give up Paula: it was not only for my present good as well as future happiness, but also for His glory. However, it still hurt.

God is such a loving provider. Trusting Him to know what is best and following His guidelines will maximize your happiness and meet your need for love every time. It wasn't until several years later that I truly understood this principle. Breaking off my relationship with Paula greatly tested my faith at the time to believe that God knew what He was doing and was reserving His best for me. But when I met and married Dottie, I learned that God *had* reserved the best for last. I wouldn't trade my relationship with my wife for anything. She's just what I need—God's perfect provision for me.

I call Psalms the praise book on God's abilities and character. In Psalm 145 David clearly declares God's motivation to provide for you and protect you. Read it and see how it expresses God's loving intent. I'm selecting key verses to show you what I mean.

Protection (v. 14): "The Lord sustains all who fall, And raises up all who are bowed down."

Provision (vv. 15,16): "The eyes of all look to Thee, And Thou dost give them their food in due time. Thou dost open Thy hand, And dost satisfy the desire of every living thing."

Protection (v. 18): "The Lord is near to all who call upon Him, To all who call upon Him in truth."

Provision (vv. 19,20): ". . . He will also hear their cry and will save them. The Lord keeps all who love Him; But all the wicked, He will destroy."

GOD'S PROTECTION AND PROVISION:
CHOOSING OR REJECTING

Isn't it exciting to realize that God's motivation, in prohibiting certain things for you, is to protect you from destructive influences that you could never foresee? In essence, God is saying, "Josh, Dale, Karen, Dan, [your name] wait! Because I love you so much, I'm going to protect you from anything that would keep you from living an abundant life." When you understand this concept, your outlook on God's law changes. You can see a God of love who uses His law as guidelines enabling you to achieve fulfillment and joy in life. No longer do you have to chafe under what you think are restrictions that inhibit your liberty. His guidelines for life are designed to maximize your happiness.

On the other hand, when you fail to trust God as your ultimate provider and protector, eventually you will almost certainly attempt to illegitimately meet your own needs. You always have two choices: 1) trust God that He is able and willing to meet your needs; or 2) selfishly attempt to fulfill your own needs.

Choosing between the two seems easy at first. You and I, as armchair theorists, would quickly agree that trusting Christ is the best course of action. But Satan is deceitful. One of his favorite strategies is to disguise wrong choices as good ones. He obviously doesn't want you to see how sin will bring grief and sorrow into your life. No one in his right mind would purposely choose grief and suffering. So Satan distracts our attention from the evil consequences of sin, and he represents the sinful choice as appealing, irresistible, and even necessary.

King David is a classic example of one who sought to meet his own needs apart from God. You no doubt know the story of David and Bathsheba; it's one of the greatest dramas of the Bible. Under the reign of King David, the tiny nation of Israel had grown to a place of respect and prestige among her neighboring kingdoms. At the tail end of a war, while the army was sweeping the hillsides on search and destroy missions, David was at home with time on his hands. While strolling on his palace rooftop one day he saw a beautiful woman bathing next door. Lust made his heart race. He inquired about her. Her name was Bathsheba, and she was the wife of one of his soldiers, Uriah.

The story is told in undisguised detail in 2 Samuel 11. David took Bathsheba into his palace and slept with her. She became pregnant. Faced with this embarrassing situation, David tried to cover his sin. He brought Uriah home from the front lines to make it appear that Uriah was the father of the unborn child. But Uriah felt it would be wrong of him to enjoy his home and family while his fellows were camping in the open field. In devotion to his king and the cause of Israel, he slept on the palace steps. What would David do now? The king finally ordered Uriah back to the front lines, giving instructions by letter to his field general, Joab, that Uriah was to fight on the front lines, and then, with the rest of the army falling back, be abandoned to fight and die alone. The orders given to Uriah amounted to a death warrant. The execution came off as scheduled. David was then free to take Bathsheba as his wife.

Months went by. Bathsheba moved into the palace, and it looked like David was home free. Yet God wouldn't let David off the hook. God marshaled one of his prophets, Nathan, and told him to go to the palace and tell David a story about a rich man, a poor man, and a lone sheep.

Nathan told David that the rich man had great flocks of sheep, but the poor man had only one ewe which he had reared as if it had been his child, feeding it from his own cup at the table. A visitor came to the city, and instead of the rich man slaughtering one of his own sheep, he took the poor man's sheep and served it to his guest. David became angry, and burst out, "As the Lord lives, the man who did this deserves to die!" Nathan pointed his bony finger under David's nose and bellowed, "You are the man" (2 Sam. 2:16,17).

What was David's primary sin? Was it lust, adultery, deception, murder? David had surely committed all these sins. Yet, when convicted by Nathan's words David cried, ". . . I have sinned against the Lord" (2 Sam. 12:13). A strange thing to say, isn't it, after someone has committed adultery and murder? Yet David's penitential prayer in Psalm 51 echoes this same theme: "Against Thee, Thee only, I have sinned, and done what is evil in Thy sight, so that Thou art justified when Thou dost speak, and blameless when Thou dost judge" (v. 4).

David did sin against Bathsheba, Uriah, and others. But that was not his primary sin. His first sin was against God, distrusting Him as his loving provider and protector. The other sins were the consequences of his offense against God. Note Nathan's declaration of what God wanted to say to David.

> . . . "Thus says the Lord God of Israel, 'It is I who anointed you king over Israel, and it is I who delivered you from the hand of Saul. I also gave you your master's house and your master's wives into your care, and I gave you the house of Israel and Judah; and if that had been too little, I would have added to you many more things like these!" (2 Sam. 12:7–8).

God had given David everything he needed and more, and if David had needed something more, God would have even given him that. But what did David do? He quit trusting God as his provider. The Scripture clearly isolates David's sin against God. "Why have you despised the Word of the Lord by doing evil in His sight?" (2 Sam. 12:9). David despised, "counted worthless," God's provisions.

Mark it down and remember it. Whenever Satan tempts you to cross the line of God's moral boundaries with the promise to fulfill a need you feel you have, it's a lie. Any provision Satan provides is an illusion, a mirage of the reality there is in Christ. Only Christ is able truly to meet your needs.

In David's life God has given us a picture of both His mercy and the destructive consequences of sin. Even though David was restored to fellowship with God, he had to suffer the consequences of his sin. The baby that was the result of David and Bathsheba's union died; one of David's daughters, Tamar, was raped by her brother; Absalom fomented a rebellion and was killed by David's own men. Indeed, for the rest of his reign, David was haunted by bloodshed, turmoil, and conspiracy.

"Without faith it is impossible to please Him," the writer of Hebrews says (11:6). "Whatever is not from faith is sin," explains the Apostle Paul (Rom. 14:23). The root cause of sin is disbelief. And the cause of King David's tragedy was a failure to rest in, depend upon, and trust in the one Person that has promised to "satisfy the desires of every living thing."

Later, years after his taking of Bathsheba, David learned that faith in God's timing was essential to a restored, happy life, and he accepted God's timetable. The songs of David record praises to God as a faithful provider for this reason. David's experience in learning to trust God as provider and protector gives the words of Psalm 37 special significance: "Delight yourself in the Lord; And He will give you the desires of your heart. Commit your way to the Lord, Trust also in Him, and He will do it" (vv. 4–5).

This is David's answer to a joyful life of loving and being loved. *Delight, trust,* and *commit* your way to the Lord. A trust relationship with a loving God empowers you to live according to His principles of life. No, joy is not in just following rules; it is in trusting a loving God who is both willing and able to provide your needs and protect you from harm.

I didn't get married until I was thirty-two. I've always said that if you want a queen for a wife, be a king! And over the years God faithfully gave me the opportunity to apply that challenge and develop into the kind of person I needed to be as a husband. And the process isn't over yet!

As you can imagine, I dated several Christian women. I thank God for those friendships because through them I was brought closer to Christ. Yet, in dating, I had to discipline my thought-life and behavior in order to conform to God's standards for singles. As I grew older, I wondered if God really had a woman especially for me and whether God's principles for love and sex were really to be exercised only in the context of a marriage commitment. I'm glad now I held steady. My heart aches to see unmarried men and women engaging in behavior that I know will rob them of the maximum relationship that God intends for them in the area of love, sex, and marriage. What made it easier to wait was the realization, imbedded deep in my mind, that I served a God who had my best interests at heart and who would withhold from me only those things that would be harmful and destructive. I realized that, by telling me to wait, God was both providing for my best and protecting me from the devastation, heartache, and emptiness caused by sin.

Dottie loves to tell how she and I met six or seven times and I never remembered her. She says that was humbling. I can understand why, but we're both convinced now this happened because even though we were always the right ones for each other, in God's eyes neither one of us was ready for a permanent relationship. The first time we met I had just returned from many months in Latin America and had just begun my traveling ministry in the United States. Dottie, who is seven and a half years younger than I, was just beginning to work with the Campus Crusade for Christ movement at the University of Texas. God knew we both needed more time as singles so He allowed us to meet on six more occasions before I even recognized her. Then in a crowd of over a thousand at an outdoor free speech rally, I spotted Dottie sitting on the grass in the back of a crowd, and I never forgot again. That was God's perfect timing. I believe He removed my blinders so I could clearly see the gift He had ready for me.

God's law flows from His motivation to provide for you and protect you. You may not always know why you suffer momentary deprivation in this life as a result of a restriction or limitation He has imposed. But you can always rest assured it is because God loves you. Place your faith *in Him,* and follow the prescribed principles and precepts as a way to develop your trust relationship with Him. What He withholds He withholds for your good.

8

Love in a Loveless World

Let's face it. Some biblical concepts are tough to apply. For instance, Jesus said, ". . . love one another even as I have loved you" (John 13:34). It's not easy to love as Christ loved, especially in a loveless world. Mostly, our human love is based on a condition: I'll love you if you love me. That's the only kind of love most of us know. And to be hit with the command "love one another unconditionally!" seems absurd, especially in our highly competitive society where people climb on top of and *over* their friends in a mad scramble up the ladder of success. Clearly, human strategies for implementing divine instructions on love aren't likely to work. God's plan for love in human relationships works on His principles, or not at all.

Remember Karen and Dan? Let's recap their situation. Karen had looked to their marriage as the be-all and end-all. She had imagined, prior to marriage, that within their own relationship she and Dan would find enough friendship and romance to satisfy their longing to give and receive love. However, Dan involved them in a whirlwind social life, which included a lot of flirting on his part with other women. Karen, because of deep insecurity, depended on Dan's fulfilling her need for love, but she was continually anxious about being betrayed. The amorous attention Dan paid other women at parties whipped these fears; she, in turn, put more and more pressure on Dan to love her and her only. Dan thought her demands were not only inappropriate but unbiblical. As a submissive wife, he reasoned, she should understand his desire to be liked and respected by their friends. Even so, he tried to meet his wife's demands, but he only bottled up for a time the impulse that led him to seek a non-stop social life and its not-quite-innocent pleasures. In the end he had become involved in a short affair, making up for lost time. And that's when Karen came to see us.

The devastating pain of Dan's betrayal was to be seen in the tears that welled up so quickly in Karen's eyes and the tight lips that barely restrained the scream that wanted to explode. At times like this, sometimes our silent presence can be of most help. Nice clichés and ready advice sound empty and cheap in the face of this kind of heartache. Waiting for the right moment to speak, I inwardly recoiled from the situation, particularly because the advice my wife and I were about to share would surely smart. Karen had to know that she was partly responsible for the impasse to which her marriage had come.

When we did start to talk we reviewed the relationship between Christ and the law. We talked about Christianity being first and last a relationship with Christ, and about the fact that our faith in Him should change all our relationships. Karen accepted this too readily; she didn't understand its implications. So we went on to discuss the law—the way in which it comes from God's love and is meant to lead us back with love in our hearts to God. I stressed that God's character, which stands behind the law and is love, existed before the revelation of Himself He gave in the law and took preeminence over it. She wanted to know what this meant. Among other things, of course, it applied to the way in which both she and Dan thought of Christianity. They had made Christianity into just another religion, thinking of it as synonymous with its teachings. That's why, even though they thought of themselves as good Christians, they could use Scripture verses as clubs in their marital warfare.

Karen sensed what was coming and started to resist at this point. If she could not hold Dan to the letter of the law, to his obligation to love her and her only, then she would be giving up, she felt, her only strength, the leverage she had on Dan in this situation.

Then my wife and I pointed out to her, from a purely practical standpoint, that her tactics were not only proving ineffectual but were actually driving Dan further from her. By treating Christianity as if it were first a set of teachings, a code of behavior, she was choking the life out of her marriage. Dan had to be free to respond to her willingly, for love can never be demanded but only nurtured. One must have the *free* choice to love or one does not love at all. Karen finally had to admit that the more she tried to force Dan to obey God's rules, the guiltier she felt and the worse the relationship became.

So what should she do? She had to begin again to love Dan, and to love him as God loves us. God's love for us in Christ models this type of no-strings-attached kind of love. "God demonstrated His own love toward us," the Apostle Paul tells us, "in that while we were yet sinners, Christ died for us" (Rom. 5:8). God doesn't demand, harangue, or threaten us if we don't respond to his overtures. He continues to draw us by the compelling force of his unquenchable love. Only as we imitate this model of love can we ever achieve God's kind of love or get the same results. It's what you might call "love, period," or, to use the Greek word, *agape.* From a psychological slant you can also call it unconditional love. This love considers the other person's needs first, even when one's own needs are greater. It complements friendship and romance with the power to give and keep on giving even when the other is unloving. It makes no demands. It is infinitely patient.

Karen's error was that she knew a lot about the teachings of Christianity, but, like most of us, not enough about the Teacher. Karen needed to "turn her eyes upon Jesus" again, and let the things of this earth, her own natural desires, grow dim until she was "alone with the Alone."

But how?

In Christian circles today there are two popular schools of thought that teach different ways of imitating Christ in giving love. They are at polar extremes. The first school is the Jesus-will-love-through-me camp. This school teaches passivity. You just wait for Jesus to pour His love through you. Stay still; wait; have faith in God, because you can't love at all. You are simply the conduit of God's love.

There's a lot of truth in this view. But it's only half the story, half the truth.

The other school emphasizes action. It is characterized by an I-will-do-it-all-by-myself theology. This school says that Jesus set the pace and gave us His example. So, you Christians, set your mind in gear (or gird up your loins) and do as Jesus did! The do-it-yourself theologians haul out their self-help kits, and urge us to give our all for Jesus. They point to those troubling passages in Scripture that outline our duties and responsibilities.

Which is right?

Well, they're both right. You must *cooperate* with what God wants to do through you. You must *choose* to love, yet by faith rely on God's love to be expressed through you. God has the resource, you have the will; both must be joined together. But don't be mistaken. *You're* the one doing the loving. You don't get bypassed in some mystical switchola.

Paul strikes the balance beautifully in Philippians 4:13: "I can do all things through Him [Christ] who strengthens me." Learning to love unconditionally requires God's Spirit to do through you what you can't do. You must actively cooperate in that process, though, through acting on your faith in God.

But how, practically speaking, do you cooperate with God in order to love others with His love? When Karen was ready, I suggested three basic steps to loving and feeling God's love. They are not three steps to relational bliss. These are not easy steps. There's nothing quick and easy about loving unconditionally. It requires a new way of thinking, and a new set of values founded on God's Word. But at each step along the way you will discover how faith enables you to love, what that means to you, and how that applies to your life.

The steps are:

1. Place your ultimate expectations for love in God alone.
2. Release others from binding expectations.
3. Personally accept God's provision of love through others.

Karen's main hang-up was that she didn't see how she could feel loved even when Dan wouldn't love her as he should. What she had to learn was more about the character of the God who did and always would love her.

WHERE TO PLACE YOUR EXPECTATIONS FOR LOVE

In order to follow through on the first step in loving others as God loves you, you have to immerse yourself in the knowledge of *how God loves* you.

First of all, know that His love is absolutely dependable. One of the shattering disappointments Karen experienced was that the enduring love she thought she had with Dan seemed to vanish. We all want to be assured of our loved one's commitment. But there is a love you can always count on, 100 percent of the time. Without fail. If your expectations of love are centered in God, you can be confident you will be eternally loved. This assurance is founded upon God's integrity and His power (He is omnipotent) to fulfill His promises. God's love will always be there. He never runs short of love, for His love is the beginning and end of all things, just as He is. Speaking of God's love, Jeremiah writes, ". . . I have loved you with an everlasting love. Therefore I have drawn you with lovingkindness" (31:3).

Karen had ample reason to feel pain and heartbreak because of Dan's unfaithfulness. But her unrealistic expectation that her desire for love could find its ultimate reference point in Dan compounded the problem. When Dan's love wavered, Karen was devastated. Yet, even in her pain, the objective reality was that she was still loved, and loved perfectly, by her infinite Lord.

A Love without Conditions

Again, there are no conditions to God's love. Karen knew that in her jealous, vindictive, and quarrelsome mental state, she wasn't as lovable as at other times. But Dottie and I were able to tell

her that God's love pays no attention to our present disposition.
His love says, "I love you in spite of what you may be like deep
inside. I love you no matter what changes about you. You can't
do a thing to turn my love off. I love you . . . period."

Paul speaks of this joyful reality in Romans 8:

> For I am convinced that nothing can ever separate us from His love.
> Death can't, and life can't. The angels won't, and all the powers of
> hell itself cannot keep God's love away. Our fears of today, our worries
> about tomorrow, or where we are—high above the sky, or in the deepest
> ocean—nothing will ever be able to separate us from the love of God
> demonstrated by our Lord Jesus Christ when He died for us. (Rom.
> 8:38–39, TLB).

Nevertheless, God's love is not blind. God knows everything
about you and still He loves you. Your shortcomings, your faults,
even your flagrant sins—God knows all these things and still loves
you. "And hope does not disappoint, because the love of God
has been poured out within our hearts through the Holy Spirit
who was given to us. For while we were still helpless, at the right
time Christ died for the ungodly" (Rom. 5:5–6).

God's love cannot be earned. His love isn't generated by some
quality in the person being loved; it is generated by the character
of the One who loves, God Himself. God begins loving us without
our ever doing one thing to merit His favor or concern. In fact,
your love for God is only possible because of God's prior love for
you: "We love Him because He first loved us" (1 John 4:19, KJV).
The whole life and ministry of Jesus, especially His death, as the
Apostle points out, testifies to this. Jesus' mission in life was to
love us first. It is His loving you first that frees you and motivates
you to love Him back, and in loving Him, to allow Him to rule
your life.[1]

When you believe God's love is both eternal and unconditional,
you can feel loved even when loved ones fail to love you as they
should. Karen had to claim by faith God's love for her and *act
upon that claim.*

HOW TO RELEASE OTHERS FROM BINDING EXPECTATIONS

Now don't misunderstand. It's both natural and appropriate to have expectations of others. Dan had made specific commitments to Karen. Karen had pledged herself to Dan and kept that pledge. It would be logical for her to assume that Dan would keep his word. But when Dan proved unfaithful, did Karen have the right to *demand*, as she did, that Dan hold to his original marriage vows? How could faith in God equip Karen to release Dan from her "binding" expectations?

The answer is found in two simple steps.

Making a Biblical Response to Unjust Treatment

Expectations are essentially presumptions of how someone will act or perform in a given situation. Karen's expectations of Dan were based on her belief that Dan would love her and always be faithful to her. But then Dan betrayed her. How was Karen to respond? How do you respond when someone sins against your trust? The first step is to identify a biblical response.

A proper response to injustice is not natural, nor instinctive. So to teach Karen and the rest of us what our response in these situations should be, Christ demonstrated in His own life how we should act.

> For you have been called for this purpose, since Christ also suffered for you, leaving you an example for you to follow in His steps . . . [he] who committed no sin, nor was any deceit found in His mouth; and while being reviled, He did not revile in return; while suffering, He uttered no threats, but kept entrusting Himself to Him who judges righteously" (1 Pet. 2:22–23).

Remember how we said Christ was able to respond lovingly to unjust treatment? Christ submitted to His accusers and didn't strike back in bitterness and resentment. He simply acted consistently with His nature. He gave love without demanding love in return. By an act of faith, He entrusted Himself to a Father who wouldn't let injustice go unnoticed. His Father would judge in due time.

Peter's inspired commentary lays the foundation for appropriate Christian responses in a variety of difficult relationships. He instructs all of us how we are to respond to human institutions of authority: citizens to government, servants to their masters, wives to husbands, and husbands to wives. He relates all these situations to how Christ responded when he was accused unjustly and suffered mistreatment.

> To sum up, let all be harmonious, sympathetic, brotherly, kind-hearted, and humble in spirit; not returning evil for evil, or insult for insult, but giving a blessing instead; for you were called for the very purpose that you might inherit a blessing (1 Pet. 3:8–9).

Karen had been "reviled" by Dan. She had a natural right to protest, just as Christ did. But what did Christ do? He submitted to His accusers and suffered unjust treatment because He believed His Father would eventually judge rightly. What was Karen to do?

> In the same way [the manner of Christ], you wives, be submissive to your own husbands so that even if any of them are disobedient to the word, they may be won without a word by the behavior of their wives, as they observe your chaste and respectful behavior (1 Pet. 3:1–2).

Let's focus momentarily on that troublesome word *submissive*. Dan appealed to Karen's obligation to be submissive. So many husbands, similarly, use the word in a manipulative way. A wife's submission to her husband does *not* entail being obedient to his every whim. Peter's definition of submission is the submission Christ manifested when "they hurled their insults at him, [and] he did not retaliate; when he suffered, [and] he made no threats" (1 Pet. 2:23, NIV). *The submission of wives is the same submission with* which workers, friends, and husbands are all supposed to respond to mistreatment. This submission releases the other from *selfish, binding expectations based on "rights."* It yields to injustice and returns good for evil. It requires more of a concern for the other's needs than one's own.

The way in which you can keep from placing selfish and binding expectations on others is to believe God will judge rightly and then allow the Holy Spirit to bathe you in His love. This is where faith connects with love.

Do you believe God is fair? Do you believe He judges rightly? If you believe that, if you entrust yourself to the One who will rightly judge your offender, you are free to love your offender. Note that I didn't say you would be free to *approve* but to *love* him or her. God doesn't approve of Dan's unfaithfulness and neither should Karen. God is not going to let wrong go unpunished. You and I don't have to demand our rights. God will judge those who violate our rights—it's His responsibility to settle the score, not ours. Rest your case at the bar of His righteous justice and love those who offend you, we are told. This kind of love is not easy and does not come naturally, but you do have a will, and that will can appeal to the Spirit of God for help. Christ wants you to love as He loves and He will supply the grace for you, if only you prepare your heart to accept it.

The most effective way to receive God's grace in such times of crisis is to cry for help *within the context of praise.* By the act of your will you can identify the response you desire and praise God for being not only your righteous judge, but you can also praise Him for being your loving friend, who will love through you with His supernatural love. Praise Him for being the love you need. Praise Him for loving you unconditionally. Praise Him for His example in returning love for insults and cruelty. Praise Him for being the Incarnation of that love which would, and finally will, transform all such situations. In this way praise will activate your faith to receive God's love.

Don't underestimate the value of praise. There is something

about expressing your appreciation to God in words, song, and meditation that solidifies your faith. The Book of Psalms is the Bible's hymnal of praise. The more you praise God for being who He is—a loving God who judges rightly—the more you can act upon your belief of what He is—eternal love.

Purifying Your Motives

The second step in learning not to place others under burdensome expectations is to allow the Spirit of God to purify your motives. At first, Karen could not detect an improper motive on her part. Dan was the one who was unfaithful. She had a right to demand Dan to stay true to her. Dan took the marriage vows by choice and she felt it only fair he keep them. There's nothing wrong with those expectations—unless they are laced with selfish motivations. The issue is not really the expectations as much as the motivation that generates our expectations. *Selfish* expectations bind and stifle relationships.

At this point the let-Jesus-love-through-you camp tips its scales toward error. In their sincere attempt to present God's truth, teachers who operate within this school of thought suggest we just clam up, accept what life brings us, and never speak of our rights. That sounds oh-so-spiritual until you realize that *God* says he gives us certain rights. That's clear, biblically. *God* expected Dan to love his wife and fulfill her needs by living with her "in an understanding way . . . [granting] her honor as a fellow heir of the grace of life, so that your prayers may not be hindered" (1 Pet. 3:7). The question is, on what were God's expectations of Dan based? *Why* did God demand fidelity of Dan? God's expectations for both Dan and Karen—for all of us—were and are based on His desire to protect us and provide for us. God expected Dan to love his wife faithfully *for Dan's own good.* God knows that love is most fulfilling when exercised in the context of commitment. He wanted Dan to be happy, and Karen too. It wasn't selfish for God to have this expectation of Dan; it was loving.

Similarly, our motives for expecting others to fulfill their responsibilities should be based on what is best for them—on love. Karen had every right to expect faithfulness of Dan. But her biblical obligation as a wife to hold him to his commitments should have been based on a loving concern for him. God never releases Dan, nor does he release us, from His admonitions that we live according to principle. Neither should Karen have released Dan from his obligation to love faithfully. What Karen had to do was release Dan from *selfishly* binding expectations. God's love has no strings attached. Ours must not either. Karen had to learn how to yield her personal expectations and put her husband's welfare first. She had to realize that Dan was the one in real trouble. Like King David, Dan was failing to trust God to provide sufficiently for him, giving evidence that he did not trust God to protect and provide for him. Karen had to respond to Dan on the basis of *the real problem.*

Again the issue is not our expectations, it's our *selfish* expectations. What stings our hearts, gnaws our souls, creates havoc and chaos in relationships, is the selfish motivations underlying our unfulfilled expectations. We want our loved ones to perform, shape up, or meet our needs for *our* sake, not God's. Nothing exposes our motives more quickly than for loved ones, friends, even acquaintances, not to live up to our expectations. And nothing creates bitterness, resentment or unforgiveness more quickly than unfulfilled, selfish expectations.

God loves you and He won't let you down. God will judge your offenders. He will demand their obedience; you don't need to place binding expectations upon them. Let your expectations go; release others from them. Keep faith in a just God who loves you and you will take a major step toward purifying your motives and releasing others from selfish expectations.

The hurt from Dan's unfaithfulness was replaced by genuine concern as Karen saw the consequences of Dan's sin unfold in his life. When she released him from her selfish expectations she was truly free for the first time to challenge him to live up to his biblical responsibilities as a husband. It was the loving thing to do then, for only in fidelity would Dan ever experience the wealth of love given in a solid marriage.

WHY GOD'S CHOICES CAN IMPROVE YOUR RELATIONSHIPS

Right now you may need to know you are loved for who you are; and it is painful not to sense that. God has made you with that need and most often chooses to provide for you through others. Accepting God's choices often improves your relationships because you view them as an integral part of God's plan for you. Placing your expectations for love in God alone and releasing any selfish demands on others prepares you to be content with the channels through whom God chooses to communicate His love. This also is a step of faith.

Being Content with God's Timing

God plans to meet your needs. Only, He will do so on His timetable. Often your faith is tested in whether you are willing to rest in the knowledge that God's timing is best. You may believe that God will finally institute universal justice, but you may still become anxious and dispute why He chooses to withhold His judgment of the evildoer and His mercy to the righteous. But you are not, like David again, to take matters into your own hands. God has promised to provide for you in "due time" (Ps. 145:15). Some versions overlay the phrase *due time* with the implication of "ripeness," a time that is appropriate and as if succulent by virtue of its growth or preparation.

God has a design and plan to provide for you, and waiting to follow His prescribed timetable will be in your best interest. It is rewarding to share with young people, for example, how God's principles for love, sex, and marriage imposes a sequence, which results in a timetable that—no matter how difficult to bear—is a light yoke in comparison to the effects of promiscuity. It always pays to wait, especially when God is keeping time.

Being Content with God's Choices

Being satisfied with God's provisions includes being satisfied with the channels God uses. Yet, sometimes those through whom God chooses to provide love need to change in various ways for their own good, and ours. How can this dilemma be resolved? Karen struggled in this area. She realized that if God was to provide through Dan, he would need to change drastically in his actions and especially his attitudes.

Yet Karen's attempts to change Dan by making demands were not successful. Coercion creates resistance to change, as you will remember. This is precisely where we must apply our understanding that God as the ultimate source of love perfectly loves us even though that love may be imperfectly expressed by those close to us.

I've had some say to me, "If I place my expectations in God and release binding expectations in my companion, he (or she) will never change for the better." That may be the surface appearance, but the very opposite is true. A lot of men will say, "Hey, if I loved my girl in spite of the way she looks or does things, she'd never change for the better." Yes, she would. Because unconditional love is a giving love. It is actually God's love poured through an individual, and it's so winsome, so irresistible that it draws out the best in the other person. It causes creative changes in the other person. The changes aren't demanded; they are simply a natural response to unconditional love.

In reality, you see, you cannot force another person to change. Only that person can change himself. But through Christ *you* can change *yourself.* When *you* change, when you begin to act differently to someone else, *that person begins to change.* It sounds incredible, yet it works time after time.

That is exactly what happened in Karen and Dan's case. For the first time, Karen began to release Dan from her demands. As she placed her ultimate trust in a loving God whom she believed in as her provider and protector, she was given the grace to love Dan unconditionally. Her love no longer depended on Dan's response. This motivated Dan to repent and change. This joyful solution does not always come about. Though God draws all men and women to repentance with His love, not all repent. But Karen was a beautiful, real-life example of a wife yielding her rights to God ". . . so that even if any of them [husbands] are disobedient to the word, they may be won without a word by the behavior of their wives, as they observe your chaste and respectful behavior" (1 Pet. 3:1–2).

All God's choices test our faith that God knows best. It tests our commitment to God as our loving provider. What if God chooses to postpone a provision for what seems to you an unreasonable period of time? How about God withholding indefinitely a provision that seems essential? Perhaps God has chosen a means of provision that you don't find readily acceptable. What then?

You have a choice to make. Either you chafe under the apparent injustice or rest by faith in the One who does all things well. Do you believe God is your loving provider and protector? Do you believe God loves you eternally and unconditionally? Do you believe He will rightly judge all those who violate your rights? If so, let your faith release others from selfish demands and allow God to show His love through you. Direct action in this regard will help you *experience* through faith the love of God.

As stressed earlier, the deeper your acquaintance with Christ, the more you are convinced He has your best interest at heart. God's moral boundaries are not given because God wishes to withhold any good thing from you, but to maximize your happiness. Your joy of loving and being loved is in Christ. All your expectations for love should be centered in Him. In God's time the longings of your heart will be fulfilled. Remember King David. Remember Dan. Remember how Karen found the essential connection between faith and love.

If you have not made this connection, examine God's Word deeply. Seek to know Him for who and what He is, and you will see that He is completely worthy of your trust. Paul said, "He who did not spare His own Son, but delivered Him up for us all, how will He not also with Him freely give us all things?" (Rom. 8:32).

PART III

Joy

Means Being Accepted

9

A Case Study in Rejection

If there is any problem that closely follows people's fear of not being able to give or receive love, it is the problem of low self-esteem. Sad to say, most people simply do not like themselves. Tall people wish they were shorter; short people wish they were taller. Thin people wish they were heavier; heavy people wish they were thinner. We all wish to be different in some way.

My own self-image began changing from negative to positive once I started building a healthy sense of acceptance. But that change was not the result of some pop psychological pep-talk I gave myself—a "you're a winner, you're a winner" piece of jargon said ten times each morning in the mirror. No, it was a process much more profound and much more lasting. I discovered that my acceptance was grounded in *God's* nature—who He was and who I was in Him. The knowledge of *that* truth is what really changed my inner sense of worth and value. I found a direct relationship between my *faith* in God and my acceptance of myself. When I *believed* I was truly accepted, my self-concept was affected.

While I was a student at Kellogg College, you will recall, my self-esteem was at its all-time low. At that point I thought faith was subjective, that how much faith a person had was more important than what or why one believed. But working harder to believe only led to continued failure and a lack of confidence in myself.

In continuing "my search," I discovered (much to my relief)

that faith was not subjective, but objective. True Christian faith focuses on Jesus Christ as its object and what *He* thinks of me as a person. When you know why you believe in Him, you are "persuaded that *He* is able to keep that which [you] have committed unto Him."

Mike and Sue are friends who, possibly like you, struggled with their need for acceptance. They too believed faith was subjective, and they held this view long after becoming Christians. Mike and Sue had a good marriage, an active church life, and two precocious teenage children. Mike had started his own advertising business, and the business had been growing steadily. Mike was well educated, sophisticated, and articulate. Sue married Mike before she finished her last year of college. Mike assured her she could finish and get her degree sometime after they married, but she never pursued it further. Mike was from the deep South and Sue from a New England state. They were now living in the South. Mike and Sue's social life revolved around Mike's business contacts and associates. Mike and Sue appeared to be a model couple.

But Sue was struggling deep inside with feelings of rejection that brought on periodic bouts of depression. These were usually triggered by incidents involving Mike's friends and associates, who would occasionally joke about her New England accent, or insinuate that she was not as educated as her husband. Sue so badly wanted these people to accept her, yet nothing seemed to work. In tears and frustration she asked, "Why can't people accept me for who I am? I feel like Mike's friends want me to be somebody I'm not. I just can't fit into their mold. Why can't just being me be enough?"

Charles Cooley, regarded by many as one of the most brilliant American sociologists, propagated a concept called the "looking-glass self." This view essentially states that a person's self-concept is largely determined by what he/she believes the most important person in his/her life thinks about him/her.[1]

Sue was an extreme case in point. Being a relational person, she found people—even casual acquaintances—very important in her life. What she believed Mike's friends thought about her affected her sense of acceptance. As Cooley points out, the battle for self-acceptance is won or lost in your mind. If you feed it false or misleading information, you set yourself up for feelings of rejection, as Sue did.

Mike was a distinctly different personality. Hard-working, goal-oriented, he loved a challenge and placed a high standard on his own performance. But Mike, like Sue, also struggled with acceptance.

For the past year Mike's advertising campaigns had not been effective for two major clients. Mike worked hard on their accounts, but no matter what he did, they failed. After losing his first client, he lamented: "I've done everything I know to do and it's not enough. If I lose one more account, I'm ruined." The financial pressure was great, but more than that, I sensed Mike was having an identity crisis. "I may not be a failure, but at this point I sure feel like one. I have so much riding on these two accounts. I've lost one and it doesn't look good on the other. I feel like I'm losing control. All my efforts don't seem to be enough. What am I supposed to do, Josh?"

Mike, as a goal-oriented person, had a drive to produce, achieve, and perform. It was natural for him to have a sense of inner satisfaction and gratification in knowing he had met his objectives. However, Mike allowed his faltering performance to determine his view of himself. What he believed about his ability to conduct a successful business directly affected his feelings of acceptance.

When both Mike and Sue began to examine just what they believed about themselves and why they believed it, it became clear that they based their sense of acceptance upon subjective feelings. While both had different symptoms, they both sought acceptance based on performance.

Sue's Perspective

Sue felt Mike's friends were unfair to look down on her. She often prayed, asking God's help to overcome her depression. She thought if she would believe God sincerely enough, He would answer her prayer, take away her depression, and help her be a better person.

Sue's Need

Sue needed to know and sense she was worthwhile even though she did not measure up to other people's social standards. She needed to feel accepted for the person she was, not what others thought she should be.

Sue's "Solution"

Sue believed her acceptance came largely from people. Sue often said, "I think the problem is with people. If they were more loving and would accept me as I am, I could be my own person without feeling pressured to conform. If they only would accept me for who I am, I wouldn't be so depressed."

Simultaneously, Sue worked hard to improve her personality. She wanted to be more loving and less sensitive to people's remarks. Sue reasoned that if she could be more composed during times of crisis—like the financial crunch resulting from Mike's failing business—then others would find her more enjoyable company and would accept her.

Mike's Perspective

In the wake of unsuccessful advertising campaigns, the two companies cancelled their accounts. Mike said, "I've developed such rapport with those men. Why didn't they call me or come by to talk it over instead of sending letters of cancellation?" The letters were terse, cold and unfriendly. Mike convinced himself that his "friends" were only friends because of what he could do for them. Mike felt that "if you don't put out you just won't have friends."

Mike's Need

Mike needed to know he was accepted even when his performance was poor. He needed to feel worthy even when he did not meet his own standards. He needed others to accept him as he was, rather than base their friendship on what he could accomplish for them.

Mike's "Solution"

Mike believed his acceptance largely came from what he could do. He would say, "If people would just give me the chance to accomplish my goals, rather than pull out when the going gets rough, I could produce wonders." He believed he could make each project succeed if only he were given another chance. Mike sought for God to prop up his own strength so he could do a better job next time. If only he trusted, he thought, God would enable him to be a greater success.

Would it have been possible for Mike to be rejected, even because of his performance, and still feel accepted? Could Sue have been rejected, even because of personal blind spots, and still feel accepted? Let's discover how.

10

Faith and Acceptance

Mike and Sue were like so many others: they had faith, even faith in Christ for their salvation, but that faith had never secured a sense of acceptance for them. What was wrong? If anyone should have a positive, healthy self-image, it is Christians, isn't it? God accepts us because of Christ and He loves us with an eternal, unconditional love. So where does the problem lie?

SUBJECTIVE FAITH'S EMPHASIS ON BELIEVING

The Value in Faith

Mike and Sue both believed that faith was subjective, that is, an inward, personal belief related to one's own experiences. But subjective faith places the worth of faith in the *act* of believing, as if faith is valuable in and of itself. They were caught on the treadmill of "building up" or "exercising" their faith. Yet, when faith becomes an end in itself rather than a means to an end (fellowship with Christ), it ceases to be true faith. Believing is then nothing more than "spiritualized" performance, "religious" self-effort, or "sanctified" works. The one *believing* becomes ultimately important. Then faith finds value only to the degree it is performed by the individual. This emphasis, unfortunately, leads to belief in a faulty basis of acceptance: our self-effort.

More and More Faith

Subjective faith also emphasizes the quantity of faith over the quality of faith. Both Mike and Sue thought it was important to have more and more faith in God. "Oh, if we could just believe in God *more*," they would say. But that emphasis also leads a person to believe that the more faith he can produce, the more pleased God will be (as if God can be "bought off" with the amount of faith we can muster). If Jesus had been concerned with the quantity of our faith, He would have said we needed faith the size of a watermelon rather than the size of a mustard seed (Matt. 17:20).

OBJECTIVE FAITH'S EMPHASIS ON THE OBJECT OF FAITH

Faith Has Value in Its Object

A Christian's faith is really an objective faith that emphasizes faith *in Christ* as its object. The value of faith is not in the one believing, but in the one believed—not in the one trusting, but in the one trusted. The efficacy or worthiness of faith is not in the faithfulness of the one believing, but rather in the faithfulness of the one who is believed.

Mike and Sue placed an emphasis on their inward *ability* to believe, rather than on the outward quality and ability of the One believed. They failed to see that their faith in Christ had value because of who *He* is, not because of who they were or what they could do or how much they could believe.

A Troublesome Fallacy

One of the biggest fallacies taught today is that salvation is by faith. Salvation *is not* by faith! Now, don't brand me a heretic yet; analyze that statement. If salvation is *by faith* then you don't need Jesus to be saved. You could save yourself. Simply have faith. But if by salvation you mean the forgiveness of sins and a personal relationship with God through Christ, you can never be saved by faith. How, then, are we saved? "For by grace you have been saved through faith; and that not of yourselves, it is the gift of God . . ." (Eph. 2:8). We are saved *by* grace, *through* faith, *in* Jesus. The Apostle Paul makes clear that faith does not save, but faith *in Jesus* saves, when he declares, "But now apart from the Law the righteousness of God has been manifested . . . even the righteousness of God through faith *in Jesus Christ* . . ." (Rom. 3:21–22; 26). Faith in Christ has value because Christ is who He claimed to be and died on the cross for our sins. Therefore, He is trustworthy. Christ, being the object of the Christian's faith, has all the qualities necessary to make that faith of infinite saving value. He is the one who saves us, not faith.

Faith is not some magical formula, as Mike and Sue seemed to think, insuring salvation for the person who possesses it. Every person has a nearly equal capacity to trust because it is part of our nature as creatures reflecting the image of our Creator. We all exercise a kind of faith from the moment we get up in the morning until we turn in at night. Even lying in bed requires faith. We commit our weight to it, believing the bed will hold us up until morning. But that kind of faith cannot save us nor bring us into a right relationship with God, because it does not rest in the right object.

It is the Holy Spirit who shows men and women that Christ is the only object worthy of faith. Someone may believe sincerely in another god or religion, but his faith will not save him. A person can be sincere, but sincerely wrong. Sincerity is not enough if the object is untrustworthy or inadequate.

SUBJECTIVE FAITH'S EMPHASIS ON SELF-EFFORT

Subjective faith has many detrimental consequences, such as legalism (can faith win favor with God?), unhealthy spiritual introspection (how can I develop more faith?), and being uninvolved in other people's lives (faith is private and personal, you know). By conditioning ourselves to think of what we must do to have more faith, we naturally think of what we must do to be accepted. Subjective faith predisposes our minds toward self-effort, self-effort leads to performance, and performance becomes the basis of acceptance with God and others.

Self-Effort Leads to Performance

Mike and Sue were believers. Yet, their concept of faith compounded their feelings of rejection. Each time they faced a crisis of rejection they sought for more faith to be all that God wanted them to be. Their subjective faith plunged them deeper and deeper into a vicious cycle of self-effort.

Mike was a doer. He thrived on having a goal and achieving it. Mike saw the value of faith to be in believing—believing more and more. So he exercised and exercised his faith in the hope that he would stimulate God into action. Surely God would recognize the fervent exercising of faith.

But Mike did not consider his believing to be self-effort. So when he failed to perform adequately as a father, how did he feel? He sat in my office and said, "Face it, when you don't put out, you get dumped on. I'm failing to be the kind of father I want to be for my kids. And, boy, are they letting me know what a terrible job I'm doing. But if I just keep praying and believing, I know God will help me. By the way, Josh, do you have any practical tips on good fathering?" It was more than good fathering tips Mike needed. He needed to correct his concept of faith.

Sue also performed for people, thinking she could please them to gain their approval. She was successful a good bit of the time, but some of her husband's associates had not come to accept her as she had hoped. She continued "doing" for them and feeling worse for the wear. No matter what she did, she could never do enough. Sue's subjective concept of faith, like Mike's, kept her focused on her ability to perform, and her self-concept suffered.[1]

The Problem with Performance as the Basis of Acceptance

Sue faced two alternative sets of facts on which to base her view of herself: 1) she could believe the faulty perspective of what people thought of her, or 2) she could believe God's opinion of her. Unfortunately, Sue's subjective orientation caused her to base her self-concept on the faulty, and sometimes fickle opinions of people who really did not know her or have her best interests in mind. Her subjective faith kept her from believing what Christ really thought of her—the only one who really knew her.

Sue needed to know what Christ, the most important person in her life, believed about her. But when she was told God accepted her, she felt little consolation. She did not consciously wish to reject God's objective truth about herself. But while she was still focusing so strongly on the views of others and attempting to perform for them, she was unable to believe God accepted her unconditionally.

Mike was headed for that same no-win situation, only his approach to performance was different. Mike's ability to achieve was the basis for his view of himself. As long as he could achieve—be a "success"—he could feel good about himself. Like Sue, Mike had to "produce" to prove he could measure up to his own high achievement standards. Mike's performance became an endless struggle to prove to himself that he had ability.

OBJECTIVE FAITH'S EMPHASIS ON GOD'S VIEW OF US

Mike and Sue based their self-concepts on subjectively determined conclusions. They both needed a new set of conclusions that would accurately reflect who they were and what they could truly accomplish. There is only one way to know the truth about ourselves: the objective Word of God.

Objective faith points to God's view. If God considers you acceptable and you believe what He says is true, that knowledge will affect your sense of acceptance. God says you are "accepted in the beloved" (Eph. 1:6). God says you "can do all things *through Christ* who strengthens [you]" (Phil. 4:13, emphasis mine). Do you believe it?

New facts give a bold reason to accept yourself as you truly are. Let us examine those facts.

11

Christ—Our Acceptance

It was a beautiful spring day. I drove slowly with my family through Pennsylvania Dutch country enjoying the scenery. One of my girls spotted a rare sight in today's high-tech society—an Amish farmer turning the sod of his field by horsedrawn plow. The horse's huge muscles rippled under his glistening coat as he effortlessly plowed the rich earth. We caught a musty whiff of leather and "horse" as we pulled to the roadside. Suddenly, my oldest daughter blurted out, "What is wrong with the horse's eyes, Daddy? He's got patches on his eyes." Laughingly I explained that nothing was wrong; the "patches" were blinders set on either side of the horse's eyes to block his side vision from any distractions.

Subjective faith works like blinders, keeping us from seeing the total picture. With subjective faith we narrowly focus attention on only a part of the picture, half the truth. Mike and Sue's subjective faith blinded them to God's viewpoint. They desperately needed to know what God thought of them.

Three concepts will give us a better understanding of God and ourselves: 1) our identity in Adam; 2) Christ's life; and 3) our identity in Christ. In our natural state, our sinful condition as children of Adam, God cannot accept us into His fellowship. Christ, by His atonement on our behalf, has reversed that condition. Our identity in Christ can meet our need for acceptance.

OUR IDENTITY IN ADAM

To best understand, we must go back to the very first persons to inhabit the newly created world fresh from the hand of God: Mr. and Mrs. Adam. Adam and Eve lived in free, uninhibited communion with God in their paradise world. It seemed nothing could interfere with their friendship with God. God had provided abundantly for His newly created offspring, giving them a vast garden to explore, inhabit, and maintain. However, in one corner of Adam and Eve's world God had hung a "no trespassing" sign, the one restriction on their liberty. One tree, out of all the other trees, was not to be touched.

Adam and Eve were confronted with a choice: to eat or not to eat from that tree. The simplicity of that choice belied its ramifications. By believing what God said was true, both Adam and Eve would find their identity in total dependence on God. Or, they could reject God's Word as true and choose to determine subjectively what was right. If they chose to believe God, they would be choosing right. Adam and Eve's "rightness" solely depended upon their choice to believe God. Believing God would result in righteousness.

We're all familiar with Adam and Eve's choice. Thousands of years of human misery prove that they chose to try their own way. Ever since Adam and Eve were expelled from the beautiful garden-home God had prepared for them, the human family has suffered alienation from God and rejection from one another. Everything that characterized Adam and Eve characterizes us: self-will, self-rejection, self-alienation. They became sinners and every child born since then comes into the world a sinner, separated from God (Rom. 5:12).

Not only are we separated from God; we have no hope on our own of reversing the condition. Paul says in Colossians 2:21 that we "were formerly alienated and hostile in mind" toward God. In addition, even if we wanted to change our minds toward God, our human efforts are unacceptable (Isa. 64:4). To top it off, the

Bible says that every transgression and act of disobedience will receive a just reward: judgment, punishment and hell (Heb. 2:2). We are born this way, cannot change, and will suffer eternal separation from God because of sin. We are doomed!

It is important to understand God's view of our sin. God is righteous and He will accept nothing but righteousness. He's not going to budge on that issue. God's love, as infinite as it is, cannot overlook our sin and accept us into His heaven. We are in an eternal deadlock and we need someone to reconcile us to God. In order to understand how great the cure is, we must understand how serious our disease, our condition in Adam, is.

1. The Spirit is dead to God.   Our spirit is that part of us that equips us to communicate with God. God is Spirit and "they that worship Him must worship Him in spirit and in truth" (John 4:23). When God told Adam he would die if he ate the forbidden fruit, God meant he would suffer spiritual death. When Adam sinned, though he did not immediately die physically, he suffered an immediate spiritual death and he was separated from God.

Every person born into this world since Adam, with one exception—Jesus Christ—enters separated from fellowship with God. In order to be in fellowship with God, we need a new birth, a reborn spirit.

2. The soul is alienated.   The soul is that aspect of our being known as the personality, which enables us to relate to others. The soul can be thought of as mind, will, and emotions—as our ability to think, decide, and feel. Under sin our soul is disoriented. Sin alienates us from ourselves and others (James 3:16; 4:1-3). God's plan in redemption is not only to give us a new spirit, but to restore us in mind, will, and emotions to Christlikeness (Rom. 12:2). God has given us a mind to know Him, a will to choose Him, and emotions to love Him. But sin has brought disorder and confusion to our personalities, our souls. In Adam, we are under bondage, slaves to sin, subject to sin's disorder and confusion.

3. The body is cursed. Our bodies are "fearfully and wonderfully made" (Ps. 139:14). They are incredible masterpieces of engineering and design. Adam must have been an impressive specimen of humanity, his body untainted by sin. But if you're like me, each day teaches me that I'm not like Adam. When I jog my knees hurt, my ankles throb and my feet cramp. I've had to take up walking for exercise because my body can't withstand the rigors of running. Medical professionals tell us that after the age of four, literally thousands of brain cells die daily.[1] Our bodies experience pain and eventual death, the result of sin's curse over God's creation. The entire created order, under the curse of sin, awaits restoration to pristine grandeur when Christ returns (Rom. 8:20–22).

This deadly curse of sin has made us dead to God, separated from fellowship and cursed with physical death. To continue in our identity with Adam is to identify with rebellion against God and self-alienation. Christ, who came to found a new race of men and women bound in close union with God, is the answer to our dilemma. Christ stands as a second Adam, the head of a new brotherhood (Rom. 5:14; 1 Cor. 15:45). Our identity in Christ assures us of fellowship and acceptance with God.

CHRIST'S LIFE

God saw the condition of His creation and decided to do something about it. His initiative rose purely from a heart of love. He did not have to do it. The plan called for God to send His only Son to earth to enter a race of men corrupted by sin, live perfectly, die an atoning death, and be the reconciler between God and man.

Why was Christ able to accomplish so perfectly what Adam failed so miserably in? Christ is righteous! The word *righteous* means just, right, correct; that which is correctly aligned with God. All that is out of adjustment with God is unrighteousness. Where Adam turned from right and sought self, Christ was consistently dependent on the Father, doing only what was right and pleasing to Him. "So then as through one transgression there resulted condemnation to all men, even so through one act of righteousness there resulted justification of life to all men" (Rom. 5:18).

Jesus Christ measures up to all the requirements for acceptance. Christ is in perfect harmony with God. As the Son of God, the second person of the Godhead, He is holy and acceptable.

The writer of Hebrews links Christ's sinlessness as God with His work as our representative, purifying our sins, reconciling us to God.

And He [Christ] is the radiance of His glory and the exact representation of His nature, and upholds all things by the word of His power. When He had made purification of sins, He sat down at the right hand of the Majesty on high (Heb. 1:3).

For it was fitting that we should have such a high priest [Christ], holy, innocent, undefiled, separated from sinners and exalted above the heavens (Heb. 7:26).

Christ is a worthy object of faith because He's righteous. His righteousness gives value to our faith. And subsequently, because He is righteous, we have salvation through Him. The worth of our faith is our acceptance by God on account of His righteous Son. Mike and Sue failed to see that faith *in Christ* is what made them acceptable. Their subjective believing kept them focused inwardly, to themselves. This subjective faith resulted in a performance based acceptance. They did not comprehend the significance of their acceptance in Christ nor claim it as their own.

OUR IDENTITY IN CHRIST

When you accept Christ's life, death and resurrection as yours, you become equally acceptable to God, as righteous in God's eyes as His Son.

Now all these things are from God, who reconciled us to Himself through Christ, . . . He made Him who knew no sin to be sin on our behalf, that we might become the righteousness of God in Him" (2 Cor. 5:18–21).

When you allow Jesus to be your Savior, a transaction takes place in heaven. He takes your sins upon Himself and endures the punishment for them. God forgives you, for the sake of what Christ does, and He forgets that you ever sinned at all. And the acceptance that Jesus enjoys with the Father because of His righteousness is transferred to you. You stand before God a perfect person. That's right! When God looks at you, He doesn't see anything wrong at all. In the words of our verse, we "become the righteousness of God *in Him* [Christ]."

The Apostle John depicts Christ as our attorney, our advocate, who pleads our case before God and rests his defense on his own righteous payment for our sin. ". . . And if anyone sins, we have an Advocate with the Father, Jesus Christ the righteous; and He Himself is the propitiation [righteous payment] for our sins" (1 John 2:1–2). Christ pleads our case because He loves us, and His appeal is heard because He is our righteous replacement.

By trusting Christ you become righteous as He is righteous. As before, you were identified in Adam, you are now identified in Christ. As before, Adam was your legal representative, now Christ legally represents you before the Father; now you legally participate in the full range of Christ's life.

This is hard for many Christians to grasp, but here it is! The moment you believe in Jesus Christ you are identified, in the eyes of God, with Christ's crucifixion, burial, resurrection, ascension, and seating at the right hand of the Father. There is such an identity between yourself and Christ that when Christ was crucified, you were crucified. When Christ was buried, you were buried. When Christ was resurrected, you were resurrected. When Christ was drawn up and seated in heaven, you were drawn up and seated in heaven. This does not require a subjective feeling to know it is true. God's Word tells you so. Because of Christ, you are accepted by God.

You are now a part of God's family, an heir to the throne. ". . . You have received a spirit of adoption as sons by which we cry out, 'Abba! Father!' " (Rom. 8:15). You are made "alive together with Christ (by grace you have been saved)." God has ". . . raised us up with Him, and seated us with Him in the heavenly places, in Christ Jesus" (Eph. 2:6). You are now seated with Christ as a co-occupant in the throne of God. You are now "accepted in the beloved" (Eph. 1:6) because you have been declared and made righteous in Christ. You might say that in your co-crucifixion with Christ you died to the penalty of sin. In your co-resurrection you were freed from the power of sin. In your co-ascension and co-seating you gained acceptance with God. You are accepted!

This masterful plan of salvation wins your acceptance with a Holy God. By simple faith in Christ you become an accepted child of God and an heir to the throne of God. What a glorious position!

Don't attempt to gain acceptance by performance—it's futile. Stop trying to achieve success in order to feel good about yourself—it won't work. Your acceptance does not depend upon what you can do. Your acceptance does not depend upon what people think. Your acceptance *does* depend upon what Christ has done; it *does* depend upon what God thinks.

If your faith is in Jesus Christ, there is nothing you can do to be accepted. It's already done. You can't add to it or detract from it. Your acceptance is complete. Accept your acceptance!

12

Accepting Our Acceptance

"Accept your acceptance!" A good thought, a great admonition, but accepting your acceptance by God is much easier said than done. You may see the futility of performance as the basis of acceptance. You may even realize that subjective faith places the emphasis on self rather than on Christ. But the need is to accept "a new set of facts" about yourself that goes contrary to what you have known all your life. Your childhood conditioning, mental habits, emotions, and education contribute to your concept of self.

A Challenge to Acceptance

Mike and Sue were faced with the challenge of overcoming the mental habits and emotional responses that had long ruled their ability to deal with the rejections and failures of life. The failure of Mike's business and the ensuing financial crunch brought both Mike and Sue to a test of faith. They were forced to examine what they believed about God and why. So, it simply wasn't realistic for me to sit back in my soft office chair and tell Mike and Sue, "You're acceptable now that you're Christians; go out and feel accepted." They had to ask the questions: "Where does my faith lie? In my ability to perform up to standard? Or in Christ? Do I believe what others think about me? Or do I believe what God thinks?" In answering those questions they began to see that although their ability to perform was inadequate, Christ would not fail to perform perfectly.

Mike could no longer remain in business for himself and had to seek a position with another advertising agency. Although it was difficult for him to accept his failure, he finally came to admit to himself and to God that he could not gain acceptance by his performance. At last he was able to release his grasp on self-effort and turn to examine just what he believed about himself and why he believed it. He began to see himself in a whole new light, as accepted by God because of what Christ had done, not because of what he could do.

The change of jobs for Mike was a personal crisis for Sue as well. She began to see that she had based her self-image on the opinions of people who were part of the changing circumstances of life. Mike now had new business associates and she would have new people whose approval she'd have to gain. She saw that it was futile to depend upon others for acceptance. The eternal, constant and unconditional love of God was hers through Christ. Her acceptance had been won and she received and acknowledged that acceptance.

Through the testing of their faith, Mike and Sue were able to correct their misconceptions, be strengthened in their faith, and accept with joy their new perspective of themselves and their relationship with Christ.

To accept your acceptance in Christ, to the point that you can feel accepted even when rejected by others, comes through a maturing process over a period of time. You must inform your mind and emotions with what is true of you according to God's Word. This surely is Paul's meaning when he instructs us to "be transformed by the renewing of your mind" (Rom. 12:2). You must look at life from God's perspective and not man's. Your response must be to accept, affirm, and act upon God's facts that are true of you. You *can* accept your acceptance.

ACCEPTING GOD'S VIEW AS TRUE

But that set of objective facts, as true as they may be, does not go unchallenged. At every step of your journey in this life there are at least two voices that cry out against the truth of God's Word and attempt to undermine God's authority: Satan and your past conditioning.

Satan Reminds Us of the Old Facts

Never forget that Satan marshals his forces against you to get you to doubt God's words. He repeats his original strategy with Adam and Eve. Remember the serpent's hissing words to Eve, "Ye shall not surely die"? Let these diabolical words emblazon themselves boldly on the walls of your mind. Let yourself feel a cold shudder as you contemplate the horrifying consequences of Adam's first sin. Doubting God is precisely where sin begins.

Every day of your life you are faced with a question: do you really believe in God's Word? There are no theological abstractions to hide behind. There is no psychological profile to analyze. You are either trusting God or you are not. If you are, your life will show it. Your mind will understand the meaning of trusting God. Your emotions will feel love, acceptance and security from that trusting relationship with God.

But how do you deal with emotions that have been scarred by past sin and childhood conditioning? Your acceptance in Christ does not automatically erase the memory of your past. Be assured the enemy makes every effort to see that you do not forget.

Prior to trusting Christ you were *not* acceptable to God. As nice as you may have appeared—you were sinful. The degree to which you *felt* unacceptable depended largely upon your past actions and childhood conditioning. If you're like most of us, you are aware that Satan has plenty of past facts of which to remind you. Those facts no doubt have been firmly established in your mind and emotions.

Now, what happens to those past facts when you trust Christ and God accepts you? Are they erased from your mind? Do your emotions, scarred by past sin, forget that negative conditioning? Unfortunately, no. Acceptance in Christ does not automatically eradicate the memory of the past.

We Remind Ourselves of the Old Facts

It is quite evident in my life that I have not arrived at perfection. My old habit patterns plague me, and many areas need change in my life. I am the first to admit it. Often, as with Peter when he was walking on the water, my attention becomes distracted from looking to Christ and I begin to look to myself. My imperfection is an ever-present voice reminding me of what yet needs to change. But I can say, that "though I am not what I ought to be, thank God I am not what I used to be; and by the grace of God I am not all I am going to be!"

While our spirits are reborn, we still have our old personalities. God intends to change our old patterns of thinking and feeling through a process of being conformed to the image of Christ. "For whom He foreknew, He also predestined to become conformed to the image of His Son, that He might be the first-born among many brethren" (Rom. 8:29). Our growth in Christ requires a process of bringing our minds and emotions into harmony with our new identity.

It may be difficult for you to grasp and accept the idea that God is *pleased* to use a process requiring time. Valuable lessons in Christlikeness are often learned through the process itself. Yet imperfect emotions, the product of sinful conditioning, argue with a powerful voice against the fact of your being accepted. Not understanding that God plans to use life's irritations to develop you into Christlikeness, you may allow your imperfections to convince you you're not acceptable. Don't do it! Accept the fact that your need for growth does not affect your acceptance. Growth, being made like Christ, is part of God's plan. Accept that plan.

Recently I struggled with my own acceptance because I was unwilling to forgive myself. During a conversation at a restaurant with some friends and associates, I said something that wounded a Christian brother who was sitting across from me. As I left the restaurant I was struck by how my remark must have sounded. I turned around, went back to the brother still sitting at the restaurant table, and sought his forgiveness. I said, "Jim, what I said a few minutes ago was wrong. I had no business saying it, and I had the wrong attitude. I've asked God to forgive me, but I sense I wounded you with my words. Will you please forgive me?"

Jim looked me straight in the eye and said, "I won't forgive you. Someone in your position should never have said what you said." I was taken aback. I have never had anyone say they would not forgive me. I thought he had misunderstood me and I apologized again. Again Jim refused to forgive me. I left the restaurant burdened with guilt and unreconciled to my brother.

Days went by and the incident kept coming to my mind. I would not let myself forget it. "How stupid can you be, McDowell? You know better than to say what you did. What kind of example are you for Christ? It just shows how unspiritual and immature you are. God can't use you. Your ministry is a sham. You're not what you ought to be."

But in the midst of my self-accusations and chastising, a still small voice reminded me that I was a redeemed child of God. I recalled, "There is therefore now no condemnation for those who are in Christ Jesus" (Rom. 8:1). I had not only sought God's forgiveness and received it but had also gone to my brother and sought his forgiveness.

I had a conscious choice to make: (1) look at my past sin and continue to upbraid myself about the stupidity of my wrong; or (2) look to Christ's righteousness and believe that God forgives and accepts me, even if my brother does not. The choice was mine. I acknowledged God's forgiveness, forgave myself and my brother who would not forgive me, and turned the entire ordeal over to God, asking for wisdom to minister to the need of my wounded brother.

I took all the steps I could to repair the relationship with my Christian brother by seeking his forgiveness. Though it was a year before Jim's wounded spirit was healed and our relationship restored, I felt as forgiven and accepted around Jim as if he had forgiven me. Why? Because I trusted in Christ's righteousness and accepted my forgiveness in Him.

Oh, I need to grow. I know that. You see, I'm not suggesting for a moment that we should be content with unchristlike behavior. I'm suggesting to be content that God is maturing you into a full-grown adult, in the likeness of Christ. Because you fail does not mean you're not accepted. It means your wrong response or action was just out of character with what God wants to develop in you. Growth comes when you recognize that and work to change.

If you have trusted Christ as Savior, God is at work conforming you to Christ's image. Accept God's view of you as a cleansed, forgiven, righteous child of God, and remind yourself of it daily. Many voices will tell you otherwise, and until you rest in Christ's acceptance, you will neither feel nor act like the new creature you are becoming in Christ.

AFFIRMING YOUR POSITION IN CHRIST

If then you have been raised up with Christ, keep seeking the things above, where Christ is, seated at the right hand of God. Set your mind on the things above [objectively], not on the things that are on earth [subjectively]. For you have died and your life is hidden with Christ in God (Col. 3:1–3).

The conditional phrase beginning with *if* is a "first-class condition" in this passage. It does not mean "if, and it might be true," or "if, and it's not true," but "if, and it is true." The first-class condition is there to lend emphasis. In other words, "*since* it is true that we are seated with Christ in the heavenlies, keep seeking the things above."[1] You do this when moment by moment you remind yourself that you are indeed positioned with Christ in the heavenlies. "Seeking" means to seek continuously in order to make application to your situation. When you "seek" for an aspirin in the medicine cabinet, you look for it in order to apply it to your headache. In the same way you are to seek the things above in order to apply them to your situation below. Do not be intent on the things on the earth (your circumstances) but be intent on the things above (your acceptance in Christ).

My personality is such that, when circumstances are against me, if I look at the situation, I'll give in, be timid, and withdraw. But daily I've learned to affirm my position in Christ. I am raised— you are raised—with Christ at the right hand of God.

That means you're accepted. Remind yourself of that every day— remind Satan of that every day. Don't let him forget it. When you're rejected by a friend or enemy, for whatever reason, affirm your position in Christ. Don't allow Satan to focus your mind subjectively on the old set of facts from the old sin life. Respond with the objective truth of God's Word. Memorize Ephesians 2:4– 6. Make the words personal and plant them deep within your heart. "But God, being rich in mercy, because of His great love with which He loved me, even when I was dead in my transgressions, made me alive together with Christ (by grace I have been saved), and raised me up with Him, and seated me with Him in the heavenly places, in Christ Jesus."

ACTING OUT YOUR NEW IDENTITY

What I am going to say in the last part of this section is extremely important. Read it carefully. Reread it if necessary until the truth is absorbed. I begin by stating a simple truth, not original with me, and where I got it I don't recall: "It is easier to act ourselves into a new way of feeling, than to feel ourselves into a new way of acting." On the surface that might appear to be purely a believe- yourself-into-a-winner-by-acting-like-a-winner kind of pop psychol- ogy cliché. But a closer look at Scripture reveals it to be the principle behind God's call to every Christian for obedience. Obedience to God is nothing more than acting through the Holy Spirit like the redeemed child of God you are and living out your true identity in Christ. Obedience helps you reinforce right patterns of behavior in your life, based on God's facts about you.

The Call to Obedience

Therefore, gird your minds for action, keep sober in spirit, fix your hope completely on the grace to be brought to you at the revelation of Jesus Christ. As obedient children, do not be conformed to the former lusts, which were yours in your ignorance (1 Pet. 1:13–14).

What is this passage challenging you to do? You are to get your mind ready for action. Fix your hope . . . where? Subjectively, on the old set of facts of your former living without Christ? No! On God's new set of facts about you, on the grace of God. You are to be an obedient child, not conformed to the old life but conformed to the new life in Christ.

Obedience does not produce a believer; but true belief will always produce obedience. And one's obedience will be consistent with one's belief. As a true believer, when you live like God's righteous child, your wounded emotions are powerfully convinced that you are acceptable.

One skillful counselor, Bob George, makes this point forcefully, showing how wrong thinking and acting influences our emotions. Bob is quoted extensively because of the need for a clear example of how acting and feeling affects our feelings of rejection:

> Now, emotions always follow thought. When someone is depressed, we say he has an emotional problem. But emotional problems, except in severe cases of physical abnormality, are caused by improper thinking.
>
> Emotions are only responders and have no intellect or intelligence of their own. They cannot distinguish between fantasy and reality or past, present or future. They merely respond predictably to whatever we are putting in our minds.
>
> People watching a horror movie experience fear even knowing there is no real monster in their room. If they know there is no reality to what they're experiencing, why do they feel fear? Because they are thinking frightening thoughts.
>
> Whatever we put in our minds determines our emotions. If we think of a sad situation, we'll feel sad. If we think of an angering situation, we'll feel anger. These things are true regardless of the reality of the thought.
>
> The same principles hold true regarding the past or future. Our minds can instantly recall a past situation—for example, an insult. Pondering that will produce an emotion of anger just as real as when the insult first occurred.

Once we are in the grip of an emotion, such as anger, we often begin fantasizing and projecting into the future as well.

Our thought processes go something like this: "That bum insulted me" (anger). "Come to think of it, he insulted me last week too" (past thinking, more anger). "As a matter of fact, he's always treated me that way!" (beginning to fantasize, more anger).

"Everybody treats me like dirt" (fantasizing, anger, self-pity). "People will always treat me like nothing" (jump to future, fantasizing, self-pity, anger).

Sustained thinking like this will produce depression.[2]

THE SECRET TO OBEDIENCE

The Apostle Paul gives you the secret to obedience in Romans 6:16–19. "Do you not know that when you present yourselves to someone as slaves for obedience, you are slaves of the one whom you obey, either of sin resulting in death, or of obedience resulting in righteousness [acceptance]?" (v. 16). Imagine a sixteenth-century scene. You are standing before two powerful monarchs and are free to choose to which leader you will give allegiance. You walk up to the one of your choice, drop to your knees, and proclaim, "Your wish is my command." Your new commander knights you into his army and you are sworn to protect and fight for his crown. You willingly choose to serve this king as a loyal subject. That is the imagery Paul projects in Romans by such words as *reign* (6:13), which comes from the root word for king; and *slave* (6:16), subjecting ourselves willingly to an absolute authority.[3] Now, with that concept of willingly yielding yourself by presenting yourself to a royal lord for the purpose of exercising his will, we can read the next three verses.

But thanks be to God that though you were slaves of sin, you became obedient from the heart to that form of teaching to which you were committed, and having been freed from sin, you become slaves of righteousness. I am speaking in human terms because of the weakness of your flesh. For just as you *presented* your members as slaves to impurity and to lawlessness, resulting in further lawlessness, so now *present* your members as slaves to righteousness, resulting in sanctification (Rom. 6:17–19, emphasis mine).

Do you get the picture? Paul is not saying be righteous and you will feel righteous. He is saying to submit to being a slave, a servant, a soldier; and give your allegiance to your master and king as an act of your will.

But there's a problem. What do you do when you are called upon to obey and you have no power to obey? This touches on an area that until now we haven't dealt with thoroughly: the ministry of the Holy Spirit. The Holy Spirit is available to you now to empower you for daily, victorious living. It isn't enough merely to have information. We need the ministry of the Holy Spirit to apply practically in our lives what God says is true of us.*

In chapter 7 of the book of Romans, Paul says there was a time in his life that he wanted to obey the law of God but he lacked the power to do it (vv. 18–25). Why? Paul had not then been raised to new life by the power of the Holy Spirit. He could not obey even when he had the desire to obey. How do you appropriate the power of the Holy Spirit in your life? The answer is simple but profound: by faith. And this is where faith and commitment are joined. When we consciously choose to obey, the Holy Spirit responds to that desire and empowers us to carry out God's will. Sometimes we have no other motivation to obey than the sheer commitment to the principle of obedience. And then we must walk in the power of the Holy Spirit by faith.[4]

Faith has a two-pronged meaning: "to live out" and "in accordance with." So to truly believe, one must choose to live in accordance with that belief. Obedience is incorporated into what biblical faith actually means. Believing is not mere mental consent; the root meaning of faith includes action. Belief leads naturally to action. That which the mind accepts the will must obey, otherwise

---

* See Appendix A in the back of this book for a more complete discussion of the importance of the Holy Spirit in empowering you for joy-filled living.

you are not really a believer. A believer of a truth will naturally follow his belief into action. Obedience is nothing more than faith in action.

When I joined Campus Crusade for Christ twenty years ago my ambition was to be a traveling youth speaker. There was already one traveling speaker for Crusade at that time, and he made it very clear to me that there was room for only one. It was a source of irritation to him that I believed various teachings of his were unbiblical and detrimental to the cause of Christ. Some time later, when I would not cooperate with an unauthorized policy that I knew Dr. Bright, the director, was opposed to, a few in leadership positions, including my irritated superior, found a way to remove me. Placement time came. I had been promised an assignment under the high school director to travel as a speaker in the High School Ministry. It was an opportunity I had waited for. Unknown to Dr. Bright, those brothers in leadership assigned me to Argentina. It was either go or leave the staff of Crusade.

I was shocked and hurt by this news. It was an attempt to remove me from the scene because I was a threat. Struggling with feelings of resentment, I thought, "How can they get away with this?" And then I remembered Romans 6:19: ". . . present your members as slaves to righteousness, resulting in sanctification." I was tempted to "fight" this assignment by going to Dr. Bright with the problem. But I also remembered Hebrews 13:17: "Obey your leaders, and submit to them; for they keep watch over your souls, as those who will give an account. Let them do this with joy and not with grief, for this would be unprofitable to you." I believed God wanted me to return blessing for insult. In obedience I willingly submitted to the Argentina assignment.

Now, I didn't have the power to keep from resenting the person who had caused this injustice. But in response to my obedience God the Holy Spirit took control of my emotions. I had a peace and contentment about my assignment, and I sensed God's warm personal approval of me. Oh, I was being rejected all right, and it hurt, but the momentary injustice couldn't overshadow the sense of acceptance I had from God.

Obedience opens the door for the Holy Spirit to apply to your emotions what in reality you are in Christ. Acting your way into right feelings is always the right order. Experience the peace and joy of your salvation by fixing your mind on what is true of you in Christ, responding to His will in your life. Live according to who God says you are, not according to your feelings.

If you have been mistreated lately or had someone reject you, drop on your knees to Christ, submit to the abuse and mistreatment, and call upon the power of the Holy Spirit for a righteous response. You can't produce a right response on your own—don't try. That comes through the power of the Spirit. Concentrate on presenting yourself as a servant to God and confessing your need for His power. He is there to live through you.

Faith in God is the key that unlocks the secret to your feeling accepted. Don't make it more complicated than it is. Don't look to yourself or your failures for excuses to not believe God's view of you. Don't let Satan convince you you're not who God says you are. Look to God with faith. He's your object of trust. Believe Him for who He is—a God who loves you and accepts you because of Christ's death, resurrection and seating on your behalf. Believe what He says is true and rest in it—you'll find true acceptance.

PART IV

Joy

Means Being Secure

13

A Case Study in Insecurity

There are more single parent homes in our society today than there have ever been.[1] Single parents, particularly, face pressures most others never face. Loneliness, heartache, and insecurity hang like a pall over the lives of many modern sophisticates. People grasp for any hope to ease the gnawing emptiness and gripping anxiety inside—from momentary escape to suicide.

Lisa's Story

By the time a young woman named Lisa came for counsel she was confused about the direction of her life and shaken in her faith. She had recently experienced a tragic and painful divorce; facing each day required courage. The divorce settlement required that she and her former husband sell the house for which they had worked so hard. But under the circumstances she had been glad that the house sold quickly. With her share of the money, Lisa found an adequate apartment for herself and the two children. She was still confronted with the difficult prospect of raising her seven-year-old son and five-year-old daughter alone, as well as the task of finding a new job. As a fairly new Christian she was doing her best to remain faithful to Christ, but her circumstances conspired against her fledgling belief.

Her job hunting turned into a full-time occupation, the days stretching on into weeks. The money from the house sale was dwindling. She *had* to find a job! Where was God when she needed Him most?

Just as her faith threatened to collapse, she got a job. Not a terribly high-paying one, but a job.

The pressure was temporarily relieved, and then she had a car accident. Her car, which sustained minor damage, was drivable, but the other was damaged extensively, and she was responsible for its repair. Because of her financial status, with the rent to pay, and grocery, utility, telephone, gasoline and other bills coming in, Lisa had not been able to keep up her insurance premiums. She just didn't have the money to repair the other car. What would she do?

Only hours after her accident a call came from Chad's school. The school office had discovered Lisa's move to a new school district, and her son Chad had to transfer within a week! Lisa had so hoped that he could finish up the school year at his old school. Uprooting Chad from the security of familiar surroundings, after losing a father, a home, and every other stable thing in his life, seemed totally unjust. But the school authorities wouldn't listen to reason. They had their code to abide by. Chad was crushed. He didn't want to go to another school and leave his friends and teacher; he didn't know anyone in the other school. He cried all evening. Lately, her little daughter had been waking up nights sobbing for her daddy, too. That night the children, after being comforted by their mother, finally gave in to sleep; but there was neither comfort nor sleep for Lisa.

Lisa had lost any sense of security. "Where is God?" she asked. "Doesn't He see what is happening? Why doesn't He help?"

Lisa needed to know that God had not lost control of her world. She needed the assurance that what was taking place would eventually be used for her good and for God's glory.

Many well-meaning Christians tried to comfort Lisa by reiterating that God would take care of her. They never accompanied their advice, though, with reasons why she should believe that. Lisa had been trying to hold onto a faith that believed God would come through for her, because, in her words, "God said He'd take care of me, and I believe Him." But now under the pressures of her trials, Lisa's belief in God as her protector and provider had reached the breaking point.

So often security eludes us. Life seems so uncertain. We all long for that inner stability and confidence that enables us to be content when life's trials come. We *want* to be free of anxiety that causes ulcers and turns us into bundles of nerves.

In the two previous sections we discovered the connections between faith and love and between faith and self-acceptance. Now we want to examine the relationship of faith to security. By faith we can have that security we so desire, unlocking the secret to knowing *why* God can be trusted, whatever our circumstances.

Lisa's Perspective

Lisa felt confused and insecure. She questioned God's promise to provide for her. She didn't want to be bitter about her trying circumstances, but it was hard to keep from fearing what would happen to her and her children.

Lisa's Need

Lisa needed that easiness of mind and heart that is security. She needed some evidence that God would deliver (or was delivering) on His promise to care for her even when it looked as if He wasn't.

Lisa's "Solution"

"The only thing I know to do is keep hoping God will answer my prayers," Lisa said. "I don't know what else to do." Lisa looked to God to bail her out, because she believed, after all, that God loved her and wanted to help her.

But that's only half the story. Lisa did not see the complete picture. In light of what Lisa knew about God, her faith had little to hold onto.

Yes, she believed God would provide and protect her because God was just and loving. And that's true; He would. But there's another dimension to God's faithfulness: not only God's loving intentions, but His perfect ability. Remember? In chapter two, we mentioned two qualities about God that give us a reason to trust Him: His perfect character and unfailing performance. Evidence about God provides the basis on which to believe in complete confidence that He cares and will meet needs.

Two Kinds of Faith

Lisa needed evidence to support her belief that God not only was willing, but was able, to meet her needs 100 percent of the time. The Christian's faith is not a blind faith, but an intelligent faith. It must have reasons to believe in God's perfect character and unfailing performance, or it will soon grow weary under the avalanche of adversity and circumstances that seem to say, "God doesn't care." Evidence of God's control will assure you, though the circumstances tell you differently, that God will supply your needs. You'll be able to say, "Here's the reason I believe that," and stand firm in life's most troubling times. Taking the principle of faith based on evidence (which everyone needs in order to believe in Christ), and applying it to the need for security creates a deep sense of contentment and joy. Faith needs substance to qualify as true, biblical faith.

Intelligent, knowledgeable faith is an exercise of trust evaluated by the mind, confirmed with the heart, and based upon adequate evidence or information. Simply "having faith" is not enough. Faith must be accompanied by convictions—convictions based on sufficient biblical knowledge, facts and evidence. A person without a knowledgeable faith will invariably suffer fear, anxiety, and basic insecurity. That's why the Bible so strongly urges us to study and to learn God's plan and purpose through His Word (1 Tim. 2:15).

We don't have to demand evidence. God has already provided evidence for His trustworthiness. All we have to do is examine it. Jesus went so far as to say: "If I do not do the works of My

Father, do not believe Me; but if I do them, though you do not believe Me, believe the works, that you may know and understand that the Father is in Me, and I in the Father." (John 10:37–38)

Christ invites you to investigate His works, His performance, that support His claim to be God. But notice where He intends your investigation to lead—"that you may know (continually know) and understand" who He really is. Christ wants your examination of the evidence to be an examination of *Him*. Getting to know the kind of God you serve will naturally engender trust.

The motivation in asking you to examine the evidence is not to create a "rationalistic faith" or an "intellectual" approach to Christianity. Examining evidence for faith is an adventure into a personal acquaintance with the character and ability of Jesus Christ. God wants you to know Him and to know that He is in complete control of all of life's circumstances. "Seek Me early and you shall find Me," "Ask and it shall be given, seek and ye shall find, knock and it shall be opened unto you." As you seek to know why God is not only willing, but very able, to meet every need, the Holy Spirit will enable you to rest secure in His plan for your life.

But the vital evidence that is to ground your faith must be gathered and examined. Where is the evidence that God can be trusted? How do you know that He will come through on His promises 100 percent of the time? One must gather the facts about God's faithfulness in the past to substantiate whether He always meets needs. As a result you will be encouraged to believe God more, understanding that He meets the needs of His people, even if for the moment the situation seems otherwise. If Lisa would weigh all the evidence, she would know beyond any reasonable doubt that God fulfills His promises. That means that whatever your trying circumstance may be, there is substantial evidence that gives you a basis for joy, even in the face of any momentary crisis. You could lose a job and feel secure—lose a loved one and feel secure—lose a home and feel secure—lose a relationship and feel secure. What a mind-boggling prospect to pursue!

14

Our Hope of Being Secure

When Christ declares, "Trust me, I've got everything under control," He doesn't say that in a vacuum. He says that amidst the storms of interruptions, irritations, ill treatment, disease, disaster and death, against the backdrop of His faithfulness and trustworthiness. Lisa is a modern-day example of the "wonderer," wondering if God had forgotten her, deserted her, left her stranded. But God hadn't forgotten Lisa and He doesn't forget about you and me.

God's Word gives us insight into the balance we need in using intelligent faith. Intelligent faith doesn't mean we'll understand everything. We will not always know what God is doing in a time of pain, or heartbreak, or a bewildering series of setbacks. But intelligent faith decides to believe God, and bases that trust on knowledge of the Scriptures; evidence about God's unquestioned ability to control the events of history and people's lives in times past—especially in the lives of biblical characters.

SECURITY IN GOD'S CONTROL

The Bible gives us an abundance of evidence that God controls history. The Bible is genuine, recorded testimony of God's involvement in history. God is God who "acts." When doubts assail our belief in God's sovereignty, intelligent knowledgable faith returns again and again to the ample evidence of His absolute dominion in the Scriptures. As we peer into the lives of men and women as revealed in God's Word, those who experienced God's sovereign control in their lives, we gain confidence and certainty that God will do the same for us. In this sense, the Bible is God's track record. God has given us a compendium of instruction concerning Himself through the history of His interaction with His people.

The Apostle Paul instructed the Corinthian church (and they needed instruction) on this very point. In two different places in the same chapter the Apostle drives home the preeminent point of the Old Testament: *"Now these things happened as examples for us, that we should not crave evil things, as they also craved"* (1 Cor. 10:6, emphasis mine). And again: *"Now these things happened to them as an example, and they were written for our instruction,* upon whom the ends of the ages have come" (1 Cor. 10:11, emphasis mine).

Notice in your Bible the number of historical incidents the Apostle recounts in 1 Corinthians 10:1–12 from the pages of the Old Testament.

- Israel's being led by the pillar and cloud
- The crossing of the Red Sea
- God's provision of manna
- The occasion of Moses striking the rock for water
- Israel's unbelief at not crossing into Canaan
- Israel's idolatry in worshiping the golden calf
- The erection of the bronze serpent to save the Israelites from poisonous snakes
- Korah's rebellion against Moses

All these incidents demonstrate God's involvement in the lives of His people and His ultimate sovereignty. Equally, the histories of Joseph, Samson, David, Gideon, Job, and Daniel—in fact, everything in the Old Testament—were given for us to see the hand of a sovereign God working in people's lives.

I think the hymn writer who penned these words got the point.

> O God, our help in ages past,
> Our hope for years to come,
> Be Thou our Guide while life shall last,
> And our Eternal Home.[1]

The next time you sing "O God, Our Help in Ages Past," think of 1 Corinthians 10:1–12 and rest secure in God's control. Based on the record of God's faithfulness in the past, you can confidently submit to His control both now and in the future.

The feast of Passover is one of the most meaningful traditions in the home life of a Jewish family. The family patriarch recites to the members of the family at the time of the Passover meal the remarkable acts of God in calling His people out of Egyptian slavery into the promised land. Dottie and I have attempted to revive the principle of this ancient practice in our home. During breakfast, I will either read or relate a Bible story to my children, not simply to acquaint them with the facts of the historical event, but to acquaint them with a faithful God and His ability to care for His people. I want to teach my children of God's wisdom, love, authority, righteous judgment, and power. And I know that the more my children learn of Him through history, the more they'll be able to trust Him based on their knowledge of His character and ability.

The premier example of God's ultimate power and control of events in the New Testament is Christ's resurrection. Repeatedly the Apostles pointed to the resurrection as demonstrative of Christ's kingship over life. In other words (not to be irreverent but to make the point), if God can pull that off, don't worry about what you're facing! It's peanuts compared to what God did in raising Jesus Christ from the dead.

You might be saying, "Why don't I feel secure?" For the same reason, no doubt, that Lisa felt insecure—you may be focusing on the immediate circumstances surrounding you rather than resting in God's total sovereignty. Oh, how your loving heavenly Father wants you to look at the evidence of His control in history and His ability to manage men's affairs. He wants you to trust Him, to believe that *He* is in control and that no circumstances can alter His plan for your life.

GOD'S KNOWLEDGE OF THE FUTURE

God has two attributes that assure you of His control: His omniscience (complete knowledge), and His omnipotence (ultimate power).

First, one must consider the logical impossibility of an infinite, eternal God not being all-knowing or omniscient. If He wasn't omniscient, then He would be limited by His ignorance; but He tells us in the Bible He is limitless, the Alpha and Omega, the beginning and the end. The psalmist spoke of our heavenly Father's knowledge (139:1–6).

Understanding God's omniscience is hard for us because, as creatures dwelling in time, we think solely in terms of time. But God is above and beyond all time, so that God's existence is one huge, eternal NOW. We use the term "prophecy" for God's knowledge of things that are in the future for us. But God has known the future as long as He has known the past, for He sees them simultaneously. Prophecy testifies to this. The accuracy of biblical prophecy demonstrates that God does not make reasonable guesses about what's going to happen; He knows absolutely, because, again, for Him these things are *always* happening.

Let's briefly go through three kinds of prophecy whose documented fulfillment gives us evidence of God's omniscience, and subsequently, His omnipotence, His control.

1. Old Testament Messianic Prophecy. Literally hundreds of years before Christ was born, God foretold His coming. We have in Messianic prophecy some of the most undeniable evidence of God's ability to see into the future. Within the records of ancient biblical history we have 60 major Messianic prophecies with over 270 ramifications which have all been fulfilled in one person, Jesus

Christ.[1] These provide overwhelming evidence of God's ability to see the future, and they confirm the identity of Jesus of Nazareth as God's Son, the Messiah. There are astronomical odds against the probability of all those prophecies, made hundreds of years before the time of Christ, being fulfilled in one man in history. God gave us these prophecies so we could see in their fulfillment the Lordship of Christ and the sovereignty of His Father. (For documentation of all these prophecies, see *Evidence That Demands a Verdict*, chapter 9, pages 141–77.)

2. Christ's Predictions of His Destiny. Christ's disciples believed that Jesus was their long-awaited Messiah. But they couldn't figure out what Jesus meant when he spoke of His death. They thought the Messiah would institute an earthly kingdom. They probably imagined that they were first in line for appointment to important political positions. We see both their affirmation and confusion in Peter's great confession, and in the rebuke that followed on its heels.

From that time Jesus Christ began to show His disciples that He must go to Jerusalem, and suffer many things from the elders and chief priests and scribes, and be killed, and be raised up on the third day. And Peter took Him aside and began to rebuke Him, saying, "God forbid it, Lord! This shall never happen to You." But He turned and said to Peter, "Get behind Me, Satan! You are a stumbling block to Me; for you are not setting your mind on God's interests, but man's" (Matt. 16:21–23).

Even though Jesus corrected the disciples, they still couldn't conceive of His death. And when it came they were grossly unprepared. Judas betrayed His master into the hands of His enemies; Jewish authorities pronounced Jesus guilty of blasphemy; and Pilate condemned Him to die. The disciples despaired and fell away. The most faithful of the bunch, Peter, skulked in the outer courtyard while Jesus was being tried, but when he was pointed out as a disciple of Jesus he denied his Lord three times.

Jesus had told His disciples, in essence, "This is all in My Father's

plan. I know things don't seem to be under control, but they are."
Of course, from our vantage point we know these events were all
in God's care.

For the moment it appeared to the disciples that Christ had
lost control. They were full of anxiety and frustration. If they could
have known the outcome, they would have been free of anxiety.
If they had understood God's master plan of salvation, they would
have understood the necessity of His death and resurrection. But
God never promised, nor designed, that we have advance knowledge
of His plans. He alone is the one who knows all, controls all, and
is worthy of our trust. Yet, God never leaves us in the dark, asking
us to trust in Him blindly. He asks us to trust Him in dark times
based on evidence of His complete control.

3. God's Plan for Man's Redemption. Before Adam was ever
created, God knew—and this may surprise you—that man would
sin against His creator. While God gave man the freedom to obey
or rebel, He knew the outcome. His plan for the world included
sending His Son to die as a sacrificial lamb from the very beginning.
The Apostle Peter asks us to consider this mystery in order to
appreciate fully the value of our redemption:

> Knowing that you were not redeemed with perishable things like silver
> or gold from your futile way of life inherited from your forefathers,
> but with precious blood, as of a lamb unblemished and spotless, the
> blood of Christ. *For He was foreknown before the foundation of the
> world,* but has appeared in these last times for the sake of you who
> through Him are believers in God, who raised Him from the dead
> and gave Him glory, *so that your faith and hope are in God* (1 Pet.
> 1:18–21, emphasis mine).

God never intended to allow man's sin and rebellion, and even
the opposition of Satan, to subvert His loving communion with
His creation. His purposes are always sure. As God ordained that
Christ would come before the beginning of the world, so He now
beholds and lives in the reality of our final ascension with Him
into glory.

GOD'S ALMIGHTY POWER

While we may admit that God is omniscient, how can we be sure He can carry out the rest of His plan? The battle with Satan is real, isn't it? Certainly man himself in his murderous ways constantly attempts to defeat God's purpose. But ultimately, we have to understand, God's plans are not contingent on circumstances. What seems like a fluctuating battle between good and evil to us appears, from God's perspective, finished and won. God, in fact, uses the very circumstances that appear to defeat His plan to accomplish His plan. Every seeming defeat turns eventually to His advantage. This is even a greater wonder.

God Always Overcomes His Opposition

Some three thousand years ago God made a promise to a man which seemed not only impossible but absurd. God promised Abraham he would make of him a great nation. There were three aspects to that promise, one of which made its fulfillment most unlikely. The promise is recorded in Genesis 12:1–2. I've printed it below beside its three aspects.

(1) A Land	"Now the Lord said to Abram, 'Go forth from your country, And from your relatives, And from your Father's house, to the *land* which I will show you;' "
(2) An Heir	"And I will make you a great *nation.*"
(3) A Blessing	"And I will *bless* you, And make your name great; And so you shall be a blessing . . . in you all the families of the earth shall be blessed."

Obviously, Abraham needed a son for his offspring to become a great nation, a nation through which all the other peoples of the world would be blessed. But he didn't have a son! His wife was barren. Then to make it worse, God waited to fulfill His promise until Abraham was old and his wife was well past her childbearing years. Talk about an obstacle! Abraham, at Sarah's urging, attempted to fulfill God's promises on his own by having a child with one of his servants, Hagar. He also named his butler, Eliezer, as his heir. But repeatedly God reminded Abraham that He, the Lord God Almighty, would fulfill His own promise and on His own timetable. God apparently wanted to reinforce His message that obstacles, no matter how ineradicable they may seem, are nothing to Him. God said, "Is anything too difficult for the Lord? At the appointed time I will return to you, at this time next year, and Sarah shall have a son" (Gen. 18:14).

A year later, Sarah, old enough to be a great-grandmother, bore a baby boy, Isaac, just as God had predicted. What an object lesson for Abraham and Sarah on waiting on God to fulfill His promise!

Afterwards, Abraham cooperated mightily with God in fulfilling the rest of the promise. At the Lord's bidding, he set out to offer up Isaac as a human sacrifice to the Lord. When Yahweh saw that his servant had passed this ultimate test of fidelity, He intervened, saving the boy's life and supplying a ram to sacrifice in his place. As a result the Jewish nation came into being, and from the lineage of David within it, Jesus Christ was born, in whom all men are truly blessed. Abraham has been called "the friend of God." He has stood for centuries as *the* example of a man who believed in God in spite of obstacles.

The Bible describes Abraham as an old man about to die this way: "And Abraham breathed his last and died in a ripe old age, an old man *and satisfied with life;* and he was gathered to his people" (Gen. 25:8, emphasis mine).

Abraham discovered the secret to contentment and security. His life stands as historical evidence that God is in control of your destiny. The more you examine God's control the more reason you have to rest secure in God's care for you.

God Transforms Opposition into Assistance

God has the ability not only to *overcome* opposition, but, as I've indicated, to *use* opposition to achieve His goals. This is the meaning of Psalm 76:10: "For the wrath of man shall praise Thee; With a remnant of wrath Thou shalt gird Thyself." Vance Havner, a beloved gospel preacher, has said, "When God wants a big field plowed, He makes Satan pull the plow." Beautiful! What security to know that God can transform opposition into assistance. In response we can only bow in humble acknowledgement and submission and rest in God's care.

Recall for a moment the events of Job's life. If anyone had reason to question God's power and God's ability to control events, it was Job. But near the end of his ghastly ordeal, after learning numerous key lessons about the God he served, Job made this proclamation: "I know that Thou canst do all things, And that no purpose of thine can be thwarted" (Job 42:2). What a rock to cling to!

Yet it appears that the freedom God has given man will at times hinder God from accomplishing His purpose. How does the freedom God has given us to make choices, harmonize with God's purposes, while never thwarting them? The sphere of man's freedom is extremely limited. From our perspective, it sometimes appears that man, as well as the devil, has an uninhibited run of the world, the freedom to oppose God and defeat His plans. This diagram can perhaps help us to understand the larger picture.

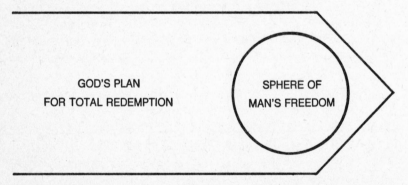

GOD'S PLAN
FOR TOTAL REDEMPTION

SPHERE OF
MAN'S FREEDOM

Man's choices never keep God from achieving His ultimate goals. His freedom will always be exercised within the boundaries set by God. Some men may resist God's plan, even fight against the current of God's will. Yet before long they will flounder in the shallows of their freedom. If you don't believe your freedom of choice is limited, try to change the events that will be recorded in the newspaper tomorrow. Or, as Jesus said, try by your own choice to grow an inch taller tomorrow (Matt. 6:27). The limits we know individually apply to mankind collectively. The sum of our freedom is infinitely less than that of our infinite God. No matter what happens when, or who does what to whom, God is still managing the world. His plan is still moving forward. From this angle of vision you can see your way to feeling secure.

A classic illustration of just how God uses opposition to accomplish His purpose is the life of Joseph. His story is documented in Genesis 37–50.

As a young man, Joseph's brothers plotted to kill him because of their jealousy of him. Through a chain of providential events, Joseph's brothers decided, instead, to sell him to the Midianites. Later Joseph was again sold to an Egyptian officer in Pharaoh's army. He worked faithfully for his new master, Potiphar, and soon rose to a position of trust and responsibility. But Potiphar's wife framed him for an affair that never took place, and he was tossed into prison. While working there he interpreted the dreams of two of Pharaoh's key men, the chief baker and butler. Two years later Pharaoh had a dream that none of his wise men could interpret. The butler remembered Joseph and told Pharaoh about him. Joseph interpreted Pharaoh's dream, and landed a job as second in command in Egypt, eventually saving Egypt and the surrounding countries from starvation during seven years of famine.

Up until this time it looked as if everything had worked against Joseph—his brother's hatred, slavery, a frame-up, imprisonment— yet all of these reverses worked in Joseph's favor. Joseph was placed in a pivotal position to save his family from starvation by bringing them to Egypt, where they quickly burst into a nation, through whom came the Redeemer. God caused every circumstance to work for Joseph's good and God's glory. Nothing came into Joseph's life that God did not use to accomplish His divine purpose.

Joseph was not blind to the evidence. He apparently came to

believe that God is able to transform the bitterest setback into a stepping stone to accomplish His goals. Joseph's evaluation of God's ability to turn opposition into opportunity is a mountain-peak statement in all of Scripture. Joseph told his brothers soon after his father's death: "And as for you, you meant evil against me, but God meant it for good in order to bring about this present result, to preserve many people alive" (Gen. 50:20).

Isn't that just like our God?

God's purposes are not always clear. Yet as Joseph accepted each circumstance into the fabric of his life as an opportunity to serve God, God's purpose unfolded. While Joseph never learned Romans 8:28 in Sabbath School he came to believe it: "And we know that God causes all things to work together for good to those who love God, to those who are called according to His purpose."

Joseph's life is evidence that God uses the very obstacles and opposition we face for our good and His glory. This is difficult to understand, I know. It often *appears* that the circumstances of life interfere with God's purpose for our lives. God allows difficulties to come, and we are faced with trials, problems and at times, serious conflicts. But has God lost control?

The Presence of Comfort

I've heard others say, in an attempt to comfort someone in trouble, "Well, it will all work out." They seem to imply that God mixes the ingredients of disappointment and sorrow up in His celestial batter, and we will only learn the proof of His intentions in this heavenly pudding long after the events which caused the pain are past.

There is some truth to that. But always looking away to some distant future may well obscure what God is doing in your life *now!* Look again at Romans 8:28. The New American Standard Bible translates it: "And we know that *God causes* all things to work out for good . . ." (my emphasis). In the original there is an emphasis on the words *all things.* The implication is that God is at work in every single event of your life to bring about your good. He doesn't overlook a single detail.[3]

That's not to say that God regards or that you should regard everything in itself as good. The results of sin, selfishness, and perversion are *not* good. God only promises to work *through* each thing in your life. No matter what its original character, if you offer it up to him, he can use it as a tool in carving out "the good" in you.

Remember Lisa? How does a knowledgeable faith help Lisa in her trying circumstances? She couldn't, for the moment, see how any good would come out of her plight. I counseled Lisa to weigh all the evidence in light of her trying circumstances. It might *not* look as if God was in control, or had her best interest at heart, but the weight of evidence of history would bear out the validity of his promise in Romans 8:28. She could rest secure, by an act of intelligent faith, in God's control.

I have to be honest with you and report that Lisa failed. The others, Karen and Dan, and Mike and Sue, took creative steps to restoration with God. Lisa, however, neglected to seriously examine the evidence regarding God's control. Her faith lacked substance, and her hopes faded. She never experienced security in the knowledge that God was working out His will in her life. Today she is a bitter, resentful, tortured woman, eaten by the haunting memories of the past. The choice was hers.

We too have a choice.

15

Security and God's Control

A very close friend went through a series of experiences that amounted to a litany of woe. Ed and his wife, Gayle, pastored a small church in a sleepy, quiet Alabama town. Their first few months were so uneventful it looked like they were in for a long, quiet ministry. Until, that is, Ed woke up one morning with a severe pain in his lower back. Aspirins, massages, hot baths, even sleeping on the floor never diminished the pain. After a few days, Ed finally went to see a doctor. The lab tests came back and the doctor delivered his verdict: kidney stones.

That was on a Friday. The doctor and his associates scheduled Ed for surgery the next Monday. The procedure was successful, and in a few days Ed was well and back at home. Unfortunately, Ed had no hospitalization insurance, so he faced a mountain of debt. The internist did waive his fee, explaining that it was his policy not to charge pastors. But the surgeon and the hospital still had to be paid.

Right after surgery, the group of churches with which Ed was associated carried out a project designed to establish a mission church on the border of Mexico. Ed borrowed the car of the denominational president to haul the group of pastors to the border. One rainy morning they needed more milk for breakfast. Ed jumped in the borrowed car, drove off, swerved around a chuckhole, spun on the mud-slick pavement, and slammed a main power pole broadside.

The trauma of the accident, carrying the additional charge of stress from his surgery, hit Ed all at once. He felt dizzy, and, as if in a nightmare, found himself weeping amidst the steaming wreckage.

"Oh, no! What have I done?" Ed buried his face in his hands. "O God, I want to die," he prayed in desperation. "I can't face Kegan with this!" But he did. And the group got safely home in a rented car.

The pastor's residence in which Ed and his family lived was located across the street from the church. Small but comfortable, it had an unusual feature: a gas furnace set in the floor covered by a metal grate. On cold mornings, hot air billowed out of the floor, warming the house.

Danae, Ed and Gayle's fifteen-month-old daughter, loved to walk across the furnace grate because of the popping, rattling sounds she created. Her mother sternly instructed her to walk *around* the furnace when it was on. She obeyed resentfully. Gayle tried to keep the baby's shoes on as much as possible as an extra precaution. A few mornings after Ed's harrowing car accident, the inevitable happened. Barefooted, little Danae walked across the furnace grate while it was going full blast. The grate was nearly red hot. Danae screamed in agony and terror. Ed and Gayle rushed their daughter to a doctor's office, where her feet were plastered with ointment and bandaged with gauze.

Gayle took Danae to the doctor twice weekly to have her feet examined and rebandaged. They were healing nicely. On the day of their second visit to the doctor, Gayle and Danae had been gone for awhile, as Ed prepared Sunday's sermon at the church. Remembering a Bible commentary he needed, Ed left his office, and crossed the street to retrieve it. The phone rang as he opened the door.

"Pastor?"

"Yes."

"Pastor, you'd better get down here. Your wife and child were just hit by a train."

Ed couldn't answer.

"Oh! They're all right, pastor. It's only the car. You'd better get down here right away, though."

Ed found a church member to take him to the railroad crossing. The crossing was rarely used and had no signal or bars to warn of an approaching train. The train, having braked and slowed, had merely nudged the back end of the car out of its way, but the pastor's Volkswagen looked as if it had been side-swiped by a charging Brahma bull.

That evening Gayle's hands shook uncontrollably. "What scares me is what could have happened," she kept repeating, rocking back and forth on the edge of her chair, her elbows close into her hips, her hands clasped against the tremors.

Kidney stones, an operation, hospital bills, an out-of-state car wreck, their baby's burned feet, the doctor bills from that, and now this nearly fatal collision with the train—all in a matter of six weeks' time! How can one feel secure in the midst of that kind of chaos?

To this day Ed and Gayle have no explanation for that quick succession of crises in their lives. Several things that came out of these difficulties were meaningful to them, however. Friends helped with their expenses—money flowed in, and Ed was able to pay the hospital bill in full before the first payment was due. This impressed Gayle in particular; her faith in God's concern for their financial situation was strengthened. It turned out the conference president got more from the insurance payoff on his car than he could probably have gotten from the trade-in on which, as it turned out, he was planning. Also, Ed and Gayle sensed a new respect for them in the community because of what they'd been through, which opened doors to their ministry. We can't know *all* the whys in this life, but God doesn't leave us without *any* answers.

Ed and Gayle were able to weather this storm because they knew God could use it to bring them closer to Him. The experience they went through can be broken down into three essential steps. These enable us to walk by a faith which knows joy even in extremity.

TRUSTING IN GOD'S CONTROL

Based on the evidence of history and God's involvement in men's lives, we must affirm our trust in God's control. That's not the same, however, as *feeling* that God is in control. The two don't necessarily go together. But by acting on the facts you know about God from the Scripture, and what you know to be true of God's sovereign control, the feelings will follow. One of the greatest expressions of faith is not asking "Why?" but "For what purpose?" God knows what is going to happen before it happens, and He plans to use it for your good and His glory. Your trust in God's control can lead you to say, like Job, "He knows the way that I take" (Job 23:10). And we can add to that, "Even if for the moment I don't."

You must realize your mind can't comprehend or know what God knows. Have you ever seen the Norman Rockwell painting of the little boy watching a baseball game through a knothole in the ballpark fence? The boy's line of sight is straight ahead. Anything to one side is out of his field of vision; anything close up is obscured. The spectators in the stands, of course, see the whole game. Your view of life is like the boy's—extremely limited. In contrast, God sees "the whole game." God sees the beginning and the end of time at once, and therefore, He holds within His mind the eternal pattern of His creation's meaning.

So what does an intelligent faith in God's control do when faced with circumstances or ill-meaning people who challenge that control? Intelligent faith examines the evidence, looks over God's track record, we might say, and decides that God has not lost control. God knows what's happening, and He is in control working out His will. *You* may not know *what* God knows, but you do know *that* He knows.

IDENTIFYING A PROPER RESPONSE

Once you affirm your faith in God's control, then you need to ask yourself, "How does God's Word direct me to act in this crisis?

What should be my reaction when trials and persecutions come my way?"

God's Word gives you the answer. Listen to God's spirit through Peter:

> Beloved, do not be surprised at the fiery ordeal among you, which comes upon you for your testing [testing of faith], as though some strange thing were happening to you; but to the degree that you share the sufferings of Christ, keep on rejoicing; so that also at the revelation of His glory, you may rejoice with exultation. If you are reviled for the name of Christ, you are blessed, because the Spirit of glory and of God rests upon you. By no means let any of you suffer as a murderer, or thief, or evildoer, or a troublesome meddler; . . . Therefore, let those also who suffer according to the will of God entrust their souls to a faithful Creator in doing what is right (1 Pet. 4:12–19).

Let's summarize the response we've examined in previous chapters:

1. Expect testing. Don't be surprised by trials and tribulations. The righteous do suffer. And God's Word teaches us to expect it: Christ, after all, wasn't spared the horror of crucifixion. He is the premier example of the righteous one who suffers unjustly (1 Pet. 3:18).

2. Keep rejoicing. God knows it is unnatural to be glad when trials swoop down upon you. So, He encourages you to rejoice. Rejoicing in the testing changes your outlook and attitude. You can begin to believe God again!—particularly if you know trials are instruments God uses (as He uses all things) for your good and His glory.

3. Do what is right. God wants your response, in both attitude and actions, to be in accordance with His character. As James writes, "Who among you is wise and understanding? Let him show by his good behavior his deeds in the gentleness of wisdom. . . . The wisdom from above is first pure, then peaceable, gentle, reasonable, full of mercy and good fruits, unwavering, without hypocrisy" (3:13,17). Allow God's Word to mold your mind, shape your attitudes, and dominate your responses. Learn new patterns of thinking—Christlike patterns—and you will experience the joy of surmounting your obstacles.

SEEKING A PURPOSE FROM GOD'S WORD

After affirming God's sovereignty, and identifying your proper response, you must seek God's purpose in your difficulties. But, you may object, didn't you just say that we can't know all the reasons, the whys for what takes place? Yes, but you can discern God's overall purpose for trials, which supplies even more evidence on which to base your faith.

Grace for Development in Christlikeness

We can speak of three basic modes of experiencing purpose and meaning in the midst of trials and persecutions.

God said He causes all things to work together for your good, remember? He went on to identify that good. "For whom He foreknew, He also predestined to become conformed to the image of His Son, that He might be the firstborn among many brethren" (Rom. 8:29).

One of God's purposes in trials is to use them to provide grace for molding you into the likeness of Christ. Seeing trials from that perspective makes all the difference in the world. God plans to use the circumstances of your daily experience to develop you in a specific direction. The "good" God wants to bring about in you is a specific good, not just generally good things. It is to specifically bring you into conformity with the character of Jesus Christ.

Patience is not my strong suit, I'll admit. But God is in the process of developing that virtue in my life; I know because I find myself far too many times painfully aware of its lack.

On one occasion when I had a very important speaking engagement in Denver, there was a need to rent a large screen for a media presentation that accompanied my address. The screen was ordered from San Francisco, and it was to be sent to Denver, and billed to my office. But because of a clerical error in San Francisco, the rental company shipped the screen to my office and the bill to Denver. When I arrived in Denver the night before my lecture, there was a phone message waiting from my office: "Where are we supposed to put the 15' x 20' screen you ordered?"

Now, without that screen, it would be difficult to give my lecture. If I didn't give my lecture, six months of planning, promotion, and organization by the local sponsors would go up in smoke, not to mention the money invested. And then, there were the over 3,300 people who had registered for the conference to consider.

The more I considered how the San Francisco screen company had bungled the order, the angrier I got. While I said nothing to anyone about my unhappiness, I felt the frustration rising. Why couldn't anyone get things straight?

When I got to my room I sat down and set out on another course of thinking. Who knew where the screen would be before it ever got there? Who ultimately controlled all the shipping companies? And who was I lecturing for in the first place? I began to think of God's sovereignty over my speaking engagements, my traveling, and over media screens. I prayed and told the Lord that this was His conference, and if He wanted me to speak with a screen, without a screen, or not speak at all, it was in His care.

As I reached for the phone to call and see what could be done, I thought of words like *rejoice, gentleness,* and *kindness.* Those were not the words in my mind five minutes earlier! But now I was bringing to mind what my response *should be.* I sat back in my chair and meditated. God has a purpose here, I mused. I'm not sure if He wants to cancel my meeting or not. But I know He wants me to be like Him. He desires that I "suffer long and be kind," that I have the virtue of patience. I lifted my thoughts to God in praise for His interest in me, for controlling and ordering the steps of my life. The more I praised Him, the more I rested my case in His care. I called my office, and asked them to send the screen to me by air freight. It arrived at the Denver airport early that next morning, the morning of the conference. The San Francisco firm apologized for the inconvenience and paid for the air freight charges. The conference went on as planned.

All our problems don't always end happily like that, and I don't always respond to a situation the same way. But, the principle is the same. God desires to restore us to complete Christlikeness, and our faith is the force that unleashes God's grace for growth.

Two key words in the passage from Romans 8:29 need to be highlighted: *conformed* and *image.*

Conformed signifies an inward, essential change of character.[1] *Conformed* comes from the same root word used in Romans 12:2 where it's translated *transformed:* "And do not be conformed [not the same word] to this world, but be *transformed* [the same word: signifying an inward change of character] by the renewing of your mind, that you may prove what the will of God is, that which is good and acceptable and perfect." The word translated as either "conformed" or "transformed" comes from the Greek *metamorphoō.* Scientists get the word *metamorphosis* from this Greek word, which describes the total transformation a caterpillar undergoes in changing into a butterfly.[2]

Image comes from the word for a statue. It's important to note that a statue is three-dimensional. In Greek, a photograph, being two-dimensional, would require the word for a *"likeness,"* while only a sculpture could be identified with the word the Greeks use for a *representation.*[3] When the Greeks spoke of a representation they had in mind the highest possible degree of imitation in another form.

Paul says God's plan is to change us into "an exact representation of Christ." One fine expositor comments on the Apostle's wording: ". . . believers are . . . to represent, not something like Him, but what He is in Himself, both in His spiritual body and in His moral character."[4]

We may be reminded, in this regard, of Paul's words regarding the process of the believer becoming like Christ: "But we all, with unveiled face beholding as in a mirror the glory of the Lord, are being transformed [inward, essential change of character] into the same image [exact representation] from glory to glory, just as from the Lord, the Spirit" (2 Cor. 3:18).

The process of becoming Christlike is accomplished by the indwelling presence of the Holy Spirit. You are being made into a new person, a part of God's new race, with Christ as the head of that new nation. But this is a process; we're statues now, but one day we will undergo a complete metamorphosis, and "this mortal shall put on immortality."

With his characteristic wit, C. S. Lewis says regarding the process of our change into Christlikeness: "And that is what Christianity is all about. This world is a great sculptor's shop. We are the statues and there is a rumor going round the shop that some of us are some day going to come to life."[5]

But let me confess, I do not always know what areas of my life God desires to perfect in me. As I continue to yield to God's hand in each circumstance, and respond properly, He continues to fashion in me the character qualities of Jesus. While I don't always know the specific quality God wants to develop in me, there is at least one quality that seems to fit if another doesn't. Paul, the Apostle, identified this quality as the one God was fashioning in him when he didn't get an answer to his prayer for God to remove his "thorn in the flesh." While I am not certain what the thorn was, I know it was a trial to him. He had asked three times that God remove his thorn. The only reply he received from God was: "My grace is sufficient for you, for power is perfected in weakness" (2 Cor. 12:9).

What was God's purpose in the thorn other than to tell Paul He had grace for him to endure it? If for no other reason, it would serve to keep him humble: ". . . lest I should be exalted above measure through the abundance of the revelations . . ." (2 Cor. 12:7, KJV). Paul had been privileged to have insights into spiritual truth that others had not had. He perceived his thorn would keep him from exalting himself. That was sufficient for Paul. He didn't have to look any further for a purpose in his trial. His final attitude was: "Therefore I am well content with weaknesses, with insults, with distresses, with persecutions, with difficulties, for Christ's sake . . ." (2 Cor. 12:10). So if you can find no other reason for a trial, you can recognize it, with Paul, as a means by which God is drawing you closer to Him, and accept it in meekness as a lesson in humility.[6]

That is probably, of course, the hardest test of all. But things as great in themselves as the test is difficult can come of it. H. W. Smith captures the essence of the Spirit's work in conforming a young woman to the image of Christ:

> The circumstances of her life she could not alter, but she took them to the Lord, and handed them over into His management; and then she believed that He took it, and she left all the responsibility and the worry and anxiety with Him. . . . And the result was that, although the circumstances remained unchanged, her soul was kept in perfect peace in the midst of them. And the secret she found so effectual in her outward affairs, she found to be still more effectual in her inward ones, which were in truth even more utterly unmanageable. She abandoned her whole self to the Lord, with all that she was and all that she had, and, believing that He took that which she had committed to Him, she ceased to fret and worry, and her life became all sunshine in the gladness of belonging to Him.[7]

Grace for Effective Service

Trials not only provide us with the opportunity to be more complete, mature people, but they also provide us the opportunity to minister to others. They give us the empathy with which to comfort others. Have you ever said to someone, "I know how you must feel," and then later thought you couldn't possibly have known how that person had felt because you never had gone through that kind of ordeal? Well, often God allows you to go through times when you don't feel loved by some loved ones, when you're rejected by friends, when some of your "security blankets" are removed, in order to provide grace for the purpose of making you more effective in ministry to others.

I can say I know what it feels like to lose a mother, who was my bellwether. I know what it's like to suffer the tragic loss of a sister by cancer. God comforted me through all that. And I have the opportunity to say in all truth to others who have lost loved ones, "I know how you feel. I've been there too."

Do you remember I shared with you my ambition to be a traveling youth speaker with Campus Crusade? Let me give the second half of that story. Without Dr. Bright's knowledge or approval some people in leadership assigned me to Argentina. It was either go or leave the staff of Crusade. I was tempted to "fight" this assignment by going over their heads to Dr. Bright with the problem. Instead I felt restrained and remembered that God had called me to minister with Crusade; and He knew in advance that the leadership wasn't perfect. I left for South America with knots in my stomach and reservations in my mind. Were these men wrong in shipping me off to Argentina? Was God really in control? However, even though I could not understand why this was happening to me, my two years in Latin America were precisely what I needed and God knew it. The experience equipped me with skills in university debates and the free speech lectures.

After God had sufficiently prepared me in spirit and mind, Dr. Bright learned of my situation and the events that led to my South American assignment. He felt the time was ripe for a work in the states similar to my university speaking ministry in South America. The group of men who had sent me into "exile" were now gone. Dr. Bright immediately called me home. From that call, my national university lecture ministry was born. While a few misguided men meant to remove me, God meant to prepare me. I learned how God uses circumstances and trials as stepping stones to more effective ways of ministry service.

Grace for Sharing in Christ's Suffering

In his well-written and insightful book *Psychological Seduction*, William Kirk Kilpatrick points out a third way in which God uses suffering for his purposes. Christianity, he says, has always maintained that in our suffering we are allowed to participate in Christ's redemptive suffering for the sake of mankind. There is still debate about this. Just how our suffering, theoretically speaking, participates in His redemptive action is difficult to understand. Yet people who have undergone great suffering in this life know something of this mystery. The biblical phrase "the fellowship of His suffering" seems to demand interpretation in such terms (Phil. 3:10), as does the passage in 1 Peter 4:12–19 which was quoted earlier. I am repeating part of the passage here to highlight a relevant and intriguing phrase:

> Beloved, do not be surprised at the fiery ordeal among you, which came upon you for your testing, as though some strange thing were happening to you; *but to the degree that you share the sufferings of Christ,* keep on rejoicing; so that also at the revelation of His glory, you may rejoice with exultation" (1 Pet. 4:12–13, emphasis mine).

The idea that in some way we share in the sufferings of Christ is clearly biblical. The degree to which we acknowledge this governs our ability to rejoice in those sufferings. "Now I rejoice in my sufferings," Paul says, "for your sake, and in my flesh I do my share on behalf of His body (which is the church) in filling up that which is lacking in Christ's afflictions" (Col. 1:24). As a believer, because you are a part of Christ's body, when you suffer, not only do you share in Christ's sufferings, but Christ suffers with you.

Christians have often alluded to this mystery of redemptive suffering in phrases like "my life for yours," and "bearing one another's burdens." Indeed, God's way of using you is many times not at all what you would have imagined or, for that matter, bargained for. Could it be that the pain you often bear, the disappointments you face, the heartbreaks you endure, are helping someone else to stand fast when all else fails? Without such a faith, in those times when God seems so far away and all you can do is endure the pain, suffering would make no sense at all.

One final word. Some teach that Christians can avoid pain, discomfort, and disease by simply "having enough faith." Nothing could be further from the truth of the Gospel than this. We are taught that we can make some sort of "claim" on God. This action of claiming becomes a matter of rigid formulas, and constitutes what in reality is a new legalism. Those who espouse these views would obligate God to jump through their faddish hoops. One or two passages of Scripture, brutally pried out of context, are used to support these contentions. But even a cursory look at the men and women of the Bible indicates that, by and large, they were not men and women free from life's trials, or who were what we would commonly regard as "successful."

No, I am not saying that God cannot heal, provide financial benefits, or perform miracles. He does, and He can. What I *am* saying is that we must acknowledge that God is sovereign in *all* circumstances. He stands above and beyond all of history, and is orchestrating the outcome as He sees fit. He may from time to time grant miraculous healings, blessings, or deliverance; but the reason these miracles occur in some people's lives and not in others is known to God alone. We are presumptuous and arrogant to presume we can know why and how these things happen.

Dr. Kilpatrick summarizes this point most eloquently.

> Suppose after putting your faith in the Lord you still have that arthritis or cancer? What then? Does it mean you haven't prayed hard enough? Does it mean something is wrong with your faith? And isn't it, finally, a form of Pelagianism—a way of thinking that God can be bought if you can ante up sufficient personal effort? That attitude, you must remember, was the one the Reformers attacked most strongly. The proper Christian emphasis is not on *our* efforts, *our* abilities, or even *our* faith. It is on our faith in *God*.[8]

To that I can only offer an emphatic "Amen!"

Epilogue: A Story of God's Faithfulness

To conclude our search in unlocking the secrets of being loved, accepted, and secure, I would like to share a period of my life that I believe illustrates how all three needs are met by faith in a God who is faithful, righteous, and all-powerful.

Have you ever experienced the pain of breaking a long-term dating relationship or engagement? You will remember my mentioning in chapter 7 that in the early years of my Campus Crusade ministry I dated a wonderful woman for three and a half years. I shared there that I loved Paula and thought she was everything I ever wanted in a wife. She was spiritually in tune with God, intelligent, articulate, gentle, and sincere. And best of all, she loved *me* and thought I was everything she wanted in a husband. We began to talk of marriage.

While directing the Campus Crusade for Christ work in Canada, God began to show me that He was going to take Paula out of my life because she was not the woman for me. Paula and I both were plagued with nagging doubts about our relationship; she told me later that she too struggled with a distinct lack of peace about our relationship but could not put her finger on the problem. But each of us hid our doubts for fear of hurting the other. Finally the turmoil became so intense that I had to share it with Paula.

I traveled down the West Coast on a speaking tour and stopped over to see her in San Diego. After I had spoken at one of the fraternities at San Diego State, Paula and I went out to a Mexican restaurant in old town San Diego. We both sensed what was coming but did not want to face it. Finally, I smiled weakly and said, "Well . . . what do you think?"

Paula burst into tears. "Oh, Josh, I feel awful," she sobbed. Seeing her in tears brought me to tears as well, realizing that God did not want us together. We decided to break off the engagement and wait and see if our feelings about God's will would change. We knew that if God wanted us together, nothing could keep us apart. That night we drove to Balboa Park and walked in the night air. It was so strange! We both knew clearly that we were not to marry, yet felt so close and dear to each other. We walked and talked until two o'clock in the morning, reminiscing over the fun times we had had and the things we had learned together about God.

The next morning Paula and her mother picked me up at my motel and took me to the airport. I stayed composed the whole time, acting as if I wasn't bothered by the break-up at all. How I hated to leave, but I knew I couldn't stay. Kissing Paula good-by was like kissing my future good-by. It seemed as if all my hopes and dreams of marriage and a family that I had secretly nurtured were shattered, destroyed, dead.

It was a long agonizing walk from the door of the terminal to the plane. I swore to myself that I'd never go through such a heartache again. It was such a temptation to turn around, run back, throw my arms around Paula and say, "Let's get married. I'll forget about Christian work. I'll go back to law school, I'll get a functional degree, start a functional practice, we'll get a functional house, have functional kids, and just function."

I literally pulled myself up the steps to the plane and upon reaching the door, began to cry. A stewardess carried my attaché bag and led me to my seat. It was one of the most difficult times of my life, and I came perilously close to cursing God and turning my back on Him. My thoughts screamed, "Why, God? You say you're a God of love? How could you take the only true love I ever had out of my life? It isn't right to be denied love. God, you can't love me and do this to me!"

Sitting on the plane, I felt my whole world was caving in. I was convinced God was angry with me and was punishing me. It seemed that He didn't want me to experience true love and didn't really care if I was ever happy.

After a couple of hours my emotions subsided and God began to work. He reminded me, "For God so loved the world that He gave His only Son"; "All things work together for good"; "I will withhold no good thing from those that walk uprightly." I began to quiet down and say, "God, I love you, I know you've called me to the ministry. And you're not taking Paula from my life because you want to punish me, but rather because you love me and have a plan for my life. You want my life to be filled with the greatest joy. It still hurts, God, but I accept your will for me. If Paula is not to be my wife, then I know you have a better plan for Paula and a better plan for me."

Right then taking a giant step of faith, I said, "God, lead on. I want to follow your design for my life. By faith I give my future into your hands. You have something better for me, not necessarily better than Paula, but better for *me* than Paula." What a lesson to learn, that God sometimes has to pry us loose from the good to give us the best.

The decision to submit myself to God's will and accept His plan for my life was made easier because of knowing *why* I believed. Trusting a God who loved me and who had proved His love for me in numerous ways was very helpful. He not only had saved me and given me purpose and fellowship with Him, but He had supplied all my needs and most of my wants. He had miraculously supplied my financial needs on several occasions; had brought me into a ministry-team relationship with a group of men and women that I dearly loved; had enriched my life through Paula's friendship and challenge to serve Christ; had provided me, through Paula's mom and dad, a model of Christian parents that I never had at home; had blessed me with all spiritual blessings in Christ; and had my life's plan and future all under control. If he had done all of this in the past, I reasoned, surely He can do something even greater in the future. I was beginning to climb out of the pit.

My faith in God wasn't blind. I was taking the facts I knew

about a faithful, loving God and relating them to my will and damaged emotions. God had not only been faithful in my life, but in Paula's life as well. God had been faithful to men and women that I knew of throughout history, and I had the record of Bible characters who had experienced God's trustworthiness. I reminded myself of the historical evidence regarding the identity, life, death, and resurrection of Christ that was so forceful in bringing me to a decision for Christ. Even in a situation in which God seemed to be nowhere near, because I could look back on all the evidence of God's love, concern, faithfulness, and trustworthiness, I knew *why* I could trust my heavenly Father.

At the time that it was clear God was taking Paula away from me, I cried, "Why, God? What have I done to deserve this? Have I sinned? Are you punishing me for something I've done?"

I felt the worst kind of rejection—rejection by God. I thought for some reason God found me unacceptable; that He was punishing me by taking Paula out of my life. I tried to make deals with God. "O God, if I pray longer and harder, can I have her back? If I go to church more, will you give her back to me? If I study my Bible more, will you let me have her then? I'll do anything to find your favor again, God." I thought God was mad at me, that He was punishing me, therefore, I thought, if I performed to please God He would give me what I wanted.

But the more I learn about God the greater confidence I have for trusting Him. If Christ is God as He claims to be and as the Bible teaches that He is, then He is able to accomplish what He said He would accomplish: my acceptance with Him. I can't improve my standing with God by religious performance, prayer, Bible reading or church attendance. My acceptance with God is already won for me in Christ. God wasn't rejecting me by withholding something wonderful from me. He was fulfilling His loving intentions toward me as my heavenly Father by giving me something better later, rather than allowing me to settle for less now.

One reason I reacted so strongly against giving up Paula was my mistaken notion that she was my last hope of love in this world. I wanted love; I needed love; and I erroneously focused my attention on a human relationship as my ultimate source of love.

Remember the first concept that Christianity is a relationship, not a religion? That relationship with God is the starting point to find love, for I will never be separated from God's love. As I acquaint myself with Him, with His character and nature as a God of love, and reflect on His eternal display of love—His death on the cross—I am reminded that I am loved by an eternal, unstoppable, unconditional love.

My faith was tested the most when I doubted God's control of my life. It was difficult to believe that a loving God would be so cruel as to rip from me the one security I had of a future of happiness and fulfillment. I had to learn that my security was in God. Because God had demonstrated His control of events within history as revealed in Scripture, and had been faithful to me over and over again, I was able to commit my future to a God who loved me, had my best interests at heart, and had the power to accomplish His will. Confidence in the Scriptures and a knowledge of His faithfulness in the past gave me an intelligent basis on which to submit my future into His hands.

It often takes time to appreciate how God works things out in our lives. Six or seven years later, when I met Dottie, I began to see how God's plan was being unfolded in my life. Even now, after thirteen years of marriage, I'm learning new dimensions of God's faithfulness. Surrounded now by a loving wife and three children, I am reminded that God loves me, Christ has won God's acceptance of me, and God is my total security in life. I now have a greater basis on which to trust God than ever before, as well as a greater basis to encourage others to trust God.

There will be times when you don't feel loved by those around you. You may feel that way now. There will be times when people reject you. And sure, life will seem topsy-turvy at times. But remember, based on what you know about God, His character and His faithfulness as an all-powerful God, you can claim the reality of the love, acceptance, and security you have in Him by faith.

ACTION STEPS TO TAKE

How can you develop a greater confidence in God, His trustworthiness and faithfulness, and His loving intentions to meet all your needs for love, acceptance, and security? There are some practical steps you can take.

1. Study the Scriptures. This should seem obvious, but most Christians don't realize the valuable library of instruction on God's faithfulness that the Bible contains. Strengthen your confidence in God by studying especially the lives of Old and New Testament men and women who experienced firsthand God's greatness, mercy, wisdom, and control. Also study the Evidence Growth Guide series, which investigates God's dealings with many Old Testament men and women. Get acquainted with the pattern of how God worked through people's lives.

2. Read Christian biographies. Purchase and read the stories of men and women who experienced God's faithfulness. Your faith will be encouraged. Here are a few biographies that have been meaningful to me:

Joni.[2] The story of Joni Eareckson and how God gave her abundant joy in the face of total paralysis.

The Hiding Place.[3] The story of Corrie Ten Boom and God's faithfulness in a German prison camp.

J. Hudson Taylor.[4] A gripping story of a man's commitment to reach the world for Christ and God's trustworthiness in answer to prayer.

Thirty Years with the South Sea Cannibals.[5] The experience of missionary John G. Patton as he reached lost men and women in out-of-the-way places for Christ.

Shadow of the Almighty.[6] The challenging life and testament of Jim Elliott, who gave his life as a martyr for Christ in carrying the Gospel to the head-hunting Auca Indians.

3. Interview mature Christians. There are many modern-day examples of God's faithfulness right near you, in your home, your church, your family, and among your friends. I encourage you to ask questions and talk to others about how God has honored His Word in their lives. You'll be motivated to trust God more as you see God working in the lives of those you know personally.

4. Be sure you're filled with the Spirit. The indwelling presence of the Holy Spirit is God's resource for bringing home to your life lessons on God's faithfulness. God's Spirit will empower you to trust more, believe more and live supernaturally as you appropriate His power by faith. I urge you, if you have not made the discovery of being filled with the Holy Spirit by faith, don't stop here, but read the Appendix that follows, take the step that I did, and appropriate the resources that are already yours through God's Spirit.

As you take these steps, and any other creative ones I'm sure you can think of, you'll have a more intelligent faith, knowing why you trust Christ as you do, and you will personally discover God's great faithfulness and trustworthiness. As you do, you'll not only be able to trust God more in trials, but in times of success you'll know to whom to pass on the thanks.

As you've discovered, unearthing principles that profoundly affect lives requires a commitment of time and energy. Anything fresh, new, alive, and relevant demands sacrifice. Since you've read this far, apparently you understand this too. Now it's time to put this book aside and apply what you've learned. Even though you and I have probed deeply into our innermost selves through these pages, all this discussion is still theoretical. Now reality begins. Be bold. Discard your former timidity, take God at His Word, and trust Him for what He claims to be and do. You've got the groundwork laid through knowing why God can be trusted. Now you have a lifetime of opportunity to do what you say you believe.

You're in for the time of your life!

Appendix: How to Be Filled with the Holy Spirit by Faith

The most effective way to explain the wonderful discovery I made of the Spirit-filled life is to share a conversation I had with Bill Bright, director and founder of Campus Crusade for Christ.

While a student at Wheaton College, I had the opportunity to have lunch with Dr. Bright. During our time together, the conversation centered on the ministry of the inexhaustible resources available to every Christian as a result of the indwelling presence of the Holy Spirit. Dr. Bright explained that something wonderful happened to the Lord's disciples on the day of Pentecost. They were filled with the Holy Spirit and went forth in His power to change the course of history.

Dr. Bright pointed out that the same Holy Spirit who empowered the disciples to live holy lives and be powerful, fruitful witnesses wants to perform that life-changing miracle in each of our lives.

The conversation that followed completely changed my view of the Holy Spirit and the power of His indwelling presence.

"The fact," continued Bright, "that Jesus Christ lives in us and expresses His love through us is one of the most important truths in the Word of God. The standards of the Christian life are so high and so impossible to achieve, that, according to the Word of God, only one person has been able to succeed. That person is Jesus Christ. When we receive Christ into our lives, we experience a new birth and we are indwelt by the Spirit. From that point on, everything we need—including wisdom, love, power—to be men and women of God and to be fruitful witnesses for Christ is available to us.

"The Christian life can be compared to the journey of a man swimming upstream against a surging current. His progress is slow and tortuous. The man can continue his attempt to swim upstream, or he can choose to board a boat with a powerful motor that can whisk him up the river effortlessly. The swimmer can always choose to get back in the water and trust his own efforts, or he can be carried along by the immeasurably more powerful boat for the completion of his journey. Such is the contrast between living the Christian life in the power of the Holy Spirit or in the energy of the flesh.

"Why do people neglect the limitless resources of the Holy Spirit and instead rely on their own efforts for living the Christian life? Many Christians are not filled—controlled and empowered—with the Spirit because of a lack of knowledge. They are fruitless and powerless simply because they do not know how to experience the power of the Holy Spirit.

"Josh," Dr. Bright continued, "there are two very important questions concerning the Holy Spirit: First, why should a Christian want to be filled with the Holy Spirit? It is impossible to live a holy life and be a fruitful witness for our Lord apart from the Holy Spirit. It is the Holy Spirit who empowers the believer for a fruitful witness. Jesus said, 'You shall receive power when the Holy Spirit has come upon you; and you shall be My witnesses both in Jerusalem, and in all Judea and Samaria, and even to the remotest part of the earth' (Acts 1:8). It is not only impossible to become a Christian apart from the Holy Spirit; it is also impossible to produce the fruit of the Spirit in our lives (Gal. 5:22–23).

"Second, how can one be filled with the Holy Spirit? Suppose that you want to cash a check for a hundred dollars. Would you go to the bank where you have several thousand dollars on deposit, place the check on the counter, get down on your knees and say, 'Oh, please, Mr. Teller, cash my check?' No, you would simply go in faith, place the check on the counter, and wait for the money which is already yours. Similarly, in asking God to fill us with

His Holy Spirit, we are asking for what is already ours by right, as children of God.

"Though you are filled with the Holy Spirit by faith and faith alone, it is important to recognize that several factors contribute to preparing your heart for the filling of the Spirit.

"First, you must hunger and thirst after God and desire to be filled with the Spirit. We have the promise of our Savior, 'Blessed are those who hunger and thirst for righteousness, for they shall be satisfied' (Matt. 5:6).

"Second, be willing to surrender the direction and control of your life to Christ in accordance with Paul's admonition in Romans 12:1,2: 'And so, dear brothers, I plead with you to give your bodies to God. Let them be a living sacrifice, holy—the kind He can accept. When you think of what He has done for you, is this too much to ask? Don't copy the behavior and customs of this world, but be a new and different person with a fresh newness in all you do and think. Then you will learn from your own experience how His ways will satisfy you' (TLB).

"Third, confess every known sin that the Holy Spirit brings to your remembrance and experience the cleansing and forgiveness that God promises in 1 John 1:9: 'But if we confess our sins to Him, He can be depended on to forgive us and to cleanse us from every wrong. And it is perfectly proper for God to do this for us because Christ died to wash away our sins' (TLB).

"Two important words spell out the steps to being filled with the Spirit. The first is *command*. In Ephesians 5:18, God commands us to be filled: 'Be not drunk with wine, in which is excess, but be filled with the Spirit' (KJV).

"The other word is *promise*—a promise that makes it possible to obey the command: 'And this is the confidence which we have before Him, that, if we ask anything according to His will, He hears us. And if we know that He hears us in whatever we ask, we know that we have the requests which we have asked from Him' (1 John 5:14–15).

"Now, Josh, as a Christian, you already have the Holy Spirit dwelling within you. Therefore, you do not need to invite Him to come into your life. The moment you received Christ, the Holy Spirit not only came to indwell you, but He also imparted to you spiritual life, causing you to be born anew as a child of God. The Holy Spirit also baptized you into the body of Christ.

"There is just one indwelling of the Holy Spirit, one rebirth through the ministry of the Holy Spirit, and one baptism of the Holy Spirit—all of which occur the moment you receive Christ. There are many fillings, as is made clear in Ephesians 5:18. In the Greek language this command of God, 'Be ye being filled,' means to keep constantly and continually being filled, controlled, and empowered with the Holy Spirit as a way of life.

"Josh," Dr. Bright probed, "have you met God's conditions for heart preparation? Do you hunger and thirst after righteousness? Have you confessed all known sin? Are you willing to demonstrate your faith by offering this or a similar prayer right now?"

Right then I prayed with Dr. Bright: "Dear Father, I need You. I acknowledge that I have been in control of my life and that, as a result, I have sinned against You. I thank You for forgiving my sins through Christ's death on the cross for me. I now invite Christ to take control of the throne of my life. Fill me with the Holy Spirit as you commanded me to be filled and as You promised in Your Word that You would do if I asked in faith. I pray this in the authority of the name of the Lord Jesus Christ. As an expression of my faith, I now thank You for filling me with Your Holy Spirit and for taking control of my life."

Then Dr. Bright confirmed God's promise. "Josh, you can be sure that God has answered you. You are now filled with the Holy Spirit whether you feel like it or not. Do not depend on emotions; we are to live by faith, not feelings, though feelings based on faith and obedience are valid, according to John 14:21."

Then Dr. Bright closed with a key thought. "Thank God each day for the fullness of His Spirit. This is your heritage as a child of God—a life of purpose, power, and fruitful witness that brings glory to our Savior. Remember, a day not lived in the fullness, power, and control of the Holy Spirit is a wasted day."

The promise of the indwelling presence of the Holy Spirit is for all of us to receive by faith. If you want it for your life, why don't you start by writing a prayer to God? Thank Him for providing His Holy Spirit to cleanse and empower your life. Then tell Him that you are trusting Him for the fullness of His Holy Spirit to pervade and control your life. Ask God to make His Holy Spirit's presence, understanding, and power in your life more evident to you. Then, daily, allow Him by faith to give you more and more of His enabling power.

In Christ you are adequate. You can accomplish all that God wants you to achieve and be. You can face life courageously and hopefully because of an expanding understanding and experience of being filled with God's Spirit. What a joy to experience having every need of our lives met by faith, resting on the solid foundation of our Lord and Savior, Jesus Christ.

Notes

Introduction

1. David Stoop, *Discussion Guide for the Sexual Puzzle* (Muskegon, MI: Gospel Films), p.2.

2. See Robert J. Stout, "Clergy Divorce Spills into the Aisles," *Christianity Today*, February 5, 1982, pp. 20–23.

3. See "The War Within: An Anatomy of Lust," *Leadership*, Fall 1982, vol. 3 no. 4.

4. See *Evidence That Demands a Verdict* (San Bernardino, CA: Here's Life Publishers, 1979).

Chapter 1

1. The testimony in this chapter is adapted from the author's book, *More Than a Carpenter* (Wheaton, IL: Tyndale House Publishers, 1977), pp. 117–128.

Chapter 2

1. Adapted from Skip Ross with Carole C. Carlson, *Say Yes to Your Potential* (Waco, TX: Word, Inc., 1983), p. 119.

2. See the authors' study manual, *Evidence Growth Guide: The Trustworthiness of the Bible*, for an in-depth study of these Bible characters. (San Bernardino, CA: Here's Life Publishers, 1983).

Chapter 3

1. Warren W. Wiersbe, *Be Hopeful* (Wheaton, IL: Victor Books, 1982), pp. 11–12.

2. Charles R. Swindoll, *Three Steps Forward, Two Steps Back* (Nashville: Thomas Nelson Publishers, 1980), pp. 85–86.

3. Wiersbe, *Be Hopeful*, p. 24.
4. Swindoll, *Three Steps Forward*, pp. 21–22.

Chapter 4
1. See Josh McDowell and Paul Lewis, *Givers, Takers and Other Kinds of Lovers* (Wheaton, IL: Tyndale House Publishers, 1980), for a full discussion of three types of love: love if, love because of, love . . . period.

Chapter 5
1. See the author's book *Jesus: A Biblical Defense of the Deity of Christ* (San Bernardino, CA: Here's Life Publishers, 1984) for more detail on the implications and scriptural proofs of Christ's deity.
2. A. T. Robertson, *Word Pictures in the New Testament*, 6 vols. (Nashville: Broadman Press, 1932), 5:186–187.

Chapter 6
1. William Barclay, *The Letters to the Galatians and Ephesians*, (Philadelphia: Westminster Press, 1976), p. 31.
2. J. Robertson McQuilkin, *Understanding and Applying the Bible* (Chicago: Moody Press, 1983), p. 259.
3. Charles Colson, *Loving God* (Grand Rapids: Zondervan Publishing House, 1983), p. 127.
4. Ibid., p. 127.

Chapter 7
1. C. S. Lewis, *Mere Christianity* (New York: Macmillan Publishing Co., 1952), p. 69.

Chapter 8
1. Peter E. Gillquist, *Love Is Now* (Grand Rapids: Zondervan Publishing Co., 1978), pp. 60–61.

Chapter 9
1. The biblical implications of this concept are explored effectively by Anthony Campolo, *It's Friday, But Sunday's Comin'*, (Waco, TX: Word Books, 1984) pp. 27–44; see also Charles Cooley, *Human Nature and the Social Order* (New York: Schocken Books, 1902), pp. 183ff.

Chapter 10
1. For further biblical principles on how to develop a healthy self-esteem, see the author's book *His Image . . . My Image* (San Bernardino, CA: Here's Life Publishers, 1984).

Chapter 11

1. Frank Minirth, "Why Christians Crack-Up," *Moody Monthly*, February, 1982, p. 13.

Chapter 12

1. Robertson, *Word Pictures*, 1:500.
2. Bob George, "There's No Need To Be Depressed," *Moody Monthly*, February, 1982, p. 7.
3. R. C. H. Lenski, *The Interpretation of St. Paul's Epistle to the Romans* (Minneapolis: Augsburg Publishing House, 1961) p. 415.
4. See Appendix for a full discussion of how to be filled with the Spirit by faith.

Chapter 13

1. *Information Please Almanac*, No. 37, 1983 ed.

Chapter 14

1. Isaac Watts, "O God, Our Help in Ages Past," 1719.
2. This has been documented in chapter 9 of the author's *Evidence That Demands a Verdict* (San Bernardino, CA: Here's Life Publishers, 1979).
3. Lenski, *Romans*, pp. 551–52.

Chapter 15

1. Robertson, *Word Pictures*, 1:227; 3:148.
2. *Webster's New Collegiate Dictionary* (Springfield, MA: G&C Merriam Co., 1975), p. 722.
3. Robertson, *Word Pictures*, 2:247.
4. Ibid.
5. C. S. Lewis, *Mere Christianity*, ibid., p. 140.
6. J. I. Packer, *Knowing God* (Downers Grove, IL: InterVarsity Press, 1973), p. 86.
7. Quoted in Al Bryant, *Climbing the Heights* (Grand Rapids, MI: Zondervan Publishing House, 1956), p. 281.
8. William Kirk Kilpatrick, *Psychological Seduction* (Nashville: Thomas Nelson Publishers, 1983), p. 193.

Epilogue

1. Available from Here's Life Publishers, P.O. Box 1576, San Bernardino, CA 92402.
2. Joni Eareckson and Joe Musser, *Joni* (Grand Rapids, MI: Zondervan Publishing Co., 1980).

3. Corrie Ten Boom with John and Elizabeth Sherrill, *The Hiding Place*, (New York: Bantam Books, 1974).

4. Dr. and Mrs. Howard Taylor, *J. Hudson Taylor*, (Chicago: Moody Press, 1977).

5. John G. Patton, *Thirty Years with the South Sea Cannibals*. Out of print but still available through libraries.

6. Elisabeth Elliot, *Shadow of the Almighty* (Grand Rapids, MI: Zondervan Publishing Co., 1958).

LET'S STAY -IN- TOUCH!

If you have grown personally as a result of this material, we should stay in touch. You will want to continue in your Christian growth, and to help your faith become even stronger, our team is constantly developing new materials.

We are now publishing a monthly newsletter called 5 Minutes with Josh which will

1) tell you about those new materials as they become available
2) answer your tough questions
3) give creative tips on being an effective parent
4) let you know our ministry needs
5) keep you up to date on my speaking schedule (so you can pray).

If you would like to receive this publication, simply fill out the coupon below and send it in. By special arrangement 5 Minutes with Josh will come to you regularly — no charge.

Let's keep in touch!

Josh

☐ **Yes!** I want to receive the free subscription to **Minutes with JOSH 5**

_____
NAME

_____
ADDRESS

_____
CITY, STATE/ZIP

Mail To:
Josh McDowell
c/o 5 Minutes with Josh
Campus Crusade for Christ
Arrowhead Springs
San Bernardino, CA 92414

SLC-2024

You've read *Evidence for Joy,* now experience ...

JOSH McDOWELL
EVIDENCE FOR FAITH
A SIX-PART FILM SERIES

This book, *Evidence for Joy,* has introduced you to evidence about God's trustworthiness. *Evidence for Faith* film series will help groups stand firm in their faith by presenting compelling historical evidence and arguments *for* the truth of Christianity and the reliability of Scripture.

1. **A Skeptic's Quest**
   Josh's personal testimony.

2. **Misconceptions about Christianity, Part I**
   Unraveling common confusions about the truth of Christianity.

3. **Misconceptions about Christianity, Part II**
   More compelling insight about the truth of our faith.

4. **The Uniqueness of the Bible**
   Evidence that reaffirms the continuity and accuracy of the Bible.

5. **The Reliability of Scripture**
   Proven methods that substantiate the Bible's authoritative claims.

6. **Messianic Prophecy**
   Biblical proof that Christ is who He says He is.

For information on how your church or organization can rent this series, call your local film distributor or call toll-free 1-800-433-3327 or, in Texas, 1-800-792-3210.

Lead a discussion group using the

Evidence for Faith

Leader Resource Kit

Provide your group with solid evidence to back up their faith, *plus* use this book *Evidence for Joy* as the resource text for the course.

Here is a 13-week curriculum designed to equip your group to answer tough questions about why they believe what they believe.

Is Christianity a blind faith?
Is the scripture reliable?
How can I be sure that Christ is the Son
   of God?
Does Christianity have any historical basis?
What about the inconsistencies in the Bible?
What is the difference between Christianity
   and other religions?

Evidence for Faith resource kit—hard facts, figures and proof of the authenticity of Christ and the Bible.

Complete kit—$29.95. Contains Leader's Guide, Student Guide, *Evidence for Joy* reading book, and two cassette tapes.

(Kit comes free with rental of *Evidence for Faith* film series.)

JOSH McDOWELL has been a traveling representative for Campus Crusade for Christ for over twenty years. A graduate of Wheaton College and a magna cum laude graduate of Talbot Theological Seminary, he is author of eighteen best-selling books, including *Evidence That Demands a Verdict, More Evidence That Demands a Verdict, The Resurrection Factor,* and *More Than a Carpenter.* He is resident instructor at The Julian Center, a rural campus in the mountains near San Diego offering a unique 3-month discipleship experience.

DALE E. BELLIS is national host for the "Six Hours with Josh" conferences and co-author of Josh McDowell's three Evidence Growth Guides. He received his Doctor of Ministry degree from Luther Rice Seminary and is a graduate of Columbia Graduate School in Columbia, S.C. He is vice-president of Evangelical Communications Corporation—an Ohio-based media production and marketing agency—where he directs curriculum development.